Mervyn Cooke
studied at the Royal Academy of Music and as a
Scholar at King's College, Cambridge, where he remained
after graduating to complete a doctoral thesis on the music
of Benjamin Britten. He was for six years Research Fellow
and Director of Music at Fitzwilliam College, Cambridge,
before being appointed Lecturer in Music at the University
of Nottingham, where he teaches courses in twentieth-cen-
tury music, jazz, ethnomusicology, film music and composition. His publications include studies of Britten's opera *Billy
Budd* and *War Requiem*, a monograph entitled *Britten and the
Far East*, and *The Chronicle of Jazz*, published by Thames and
Hudson; he is currently co-editing Britten's letters and edit-
ing *The Cambridge Companion to Britten*. He is also a pianist
and composer: his compositions have been broadcast on
BBC Radio 3 and Radio France, and performed at the
South Bank and St John's, Smith Square, in London.

WORLD OF ART

This famous series
provides the widest available
range of illustrated books on art in all its aspects.
If you would like to receive a complete list
of titles in print please write to:
THAMES AND HUDSON
30 Bloomsbury Street, London WC1B 3QP
In the United States please write to:
THAMES AND HUDSON INC.
500 Fifth Avenue, New York, New York 10110

Printed in Slovenia

Mervyn Cooke

Jazz

153 illustrations

THAMES AND HUDSON

For Mimi

1 Detail of Lee Morgan
playing the trumpet.

© 1998 Thames and Hudson Ltd, London

First published in the United States of America in 1999 by Thames and Hudson Inc.,
500 Fifth Avenue, New York, New York 10110

Library of Congress Catalog Card Number 98-60193
ISBN 0-500-20318-0

Printed and bound in Slovenia

Contents

CHAPTER ONE

Out of Africa

'Jazz', George Gershwin is reported to have said, 'is the result of the energy stored up in America.' Many commentators would substitute 'racial tension' for 'energy', and there is little doubt that America's most enduring contribution to contemporary culture evolved directly from the severe racial problems afflicting that country in the years immediately after the Civil War (1861–65). The story of jazz is one of the extraordinary relationship between black and white people: white musicians copying black styles for commercial gain, black musicians regaining the creative initiative for themselves and injecting 'their' music with aggressive political symbolism, and musicians of both colours playing alongside one another in racial and musical harmony. In this last respect jazz has, from its earliest years, been one of the most potent cultural forces in the United States, and those who insist that the entire history of jazz is a tale of racial strife should not overlook the obvious fact that the vast majority of jazz is cheerful and exuberant. The development of jazz in Europe has, for historical reasons, been largely free of racial tension and American musicians perceived this stark difference in social climate on their European tours. Many were reluctant to return home; indeed, some decided not to.

This is one of jazz's richest ironies, since Europeans had been responsible for transplanting Africans to North America in the first place. There is no escaping the fact that jazz owes its origins to the slave trade, a disconcerting reminder of our imperial (and not so distant) past. From the sixteenth century onwards, hundreds of thousands of slaves were transported by European traders to the New World, where they became largely concentrated in the lucrative rice and cotton plantations of the southern states. By the early nineteenth century, slavery had become a serious bone of contention between the industrialized North and the agrarian South. Campaigners such as the British MP William Wilberforce were vociferous in drawing attention

2 A typical harvest scene on a sugar plantation in Louisiana, depicted in *Harper's Weekly* in 1875.

3 A nostalgic depiction of African drumming in Place Congo, New Orleans.

to the trade's immorality, and it was duly abolished by British Parliament in 1807, ceasing in all outreaches of the British Empire in 1833. In the United States, importation of slaves was made illegal in 1808 (by which time almost half a million Africans had been relocated), but slavery continued to flourish illicitly. The Abolition Movement grew in strength from the 1830s onwards, and it was when Abraham Lincoln became president in 1860 that dissent came to a head. Lincoln's recently formed Republican Party was vigorously opposed to slavery, and went to war over the issue against the confederacy of eleven secessionist southern states under Jefferson Davis. In 1863, during the bloody four-year Civil War, Lincoln issued his Emancipation Proclamation designed to liberate all slaves in the South. Slavery was finally abolished by the Thirteenth Amendment to the US Constitution in 1865, shortly before Lincoln's assassination.

The majority of slaves had been drawn from West African tribes with strong musical traditions, which they took with them to America. Authentic African dances continued to be celebrated at lavish festivals, such as those organized on Sundays at Place Congo in New Orleans and at similar gatherings in New England and New York, but they dwindled in the middle of the nineteenth century; the Place Congo celebrations, which had in any case been carried out under strict supervision by the police, were banned in 1843. In some areas, notably Texas, first-generation African slaves continued to arrive

8

as late as the Civil War years. Slave owners did their best to split up slaves who belonged to the same tribe, hoping to destroy their native traditions and thus prevent clandestine communication; in Georgia and Mississippi, slaves were refused access to drums or loud wind instruments for fear that these could be used to convey messages by means of musical codes. Undaunted, resourceful slaves manufactured their own instruments from readily available materials. One example was the banjo, probably based on African prototypes such as the Senegalese *bania* (which may have given its name to the new instrument). The banjo later found a temporary niche in early jazz bands until it was supplanted by the more versatile guitar in the 1930s.

The spirit of group identity and social responsibility embodied in African music survived these systematic depredations, however, and among the slaves concentrated on plantations several modified

4 In another romanticized image, a black worker tries out a banjo under the watchful eye of a white salesman.

SLAVE SONGS OF THE UNITED STATES.

I.

1. **ROLL, JORDAN, ROLL.**

1. My brudder* sit-tin' on de tree of life, An' he yearde when Jor-dan roll; Roll, Jor-dan, Roll, Jor-dan, Roll, Jor-dan, roll! O march de an-gel march, O march de an-gel march; O my soul a-rise in Heaven, Lord, For to yearde when Jor-dan roll.

2 Little chil'en, learn to fear de Lord,
And let your days be long;
Roll, Jordan, &c.

3 O, let no false nor spiteful word
Be found upon your tongue;
Roll, Jorda₁, &c.

5 This popular item in the 1867 anthology of slave songs demonstrates syncopation, a partially pentatonic melody and an editorial attempt to notate blue notes.

musical genres began to emerge. Since much African music is strictly functional, accompanying work or rituals, the most widespread development was the work song – working was, after all, how slaves spent all their waking hours. Singing was encouraged by most plantation owners, on the naive assumption that a singing slave is a happy slave. Many work songs were performed above a slow, steady rhythmical beat created by some physical activity such as clapping, footstamping or – during hard labour – the blow of an axe or other heavy implement. If drums were permitted, they might also be employed to create the underlying pulse. Black stevedores (shiploaders) working in the port of New Orleans were renowned for their fine work songs, which may have directly influenced the first generation of jazz musicians in the city. Related to the work song was the 'field holler', an improvised song of encouragement sung by a soloist and addressed to the rest of the workforce, which also evolved from African tribal practices. As the American folklorist Alan Lomax demonstrated in a series of tape recordings made during the 1960s, the style of these ritualistic work songs and field hollers survived without apparent modification among black working parties on prison farms in certain American penitentiaries, which represent perhaps the closest modern equivalent to the old plantation system. One prison song was remarkably similar in style to a native song still performed in Senegal.

The most impressive aspect of West African music is its sophisticated rhythmic organization. Especially characteristic is the technique of 'polyrhythm' in which contrasting rhythmic patterns are superimposed to create textures of considerable complexity and vitality. Deprived of drums and the society of slaves from the same tribe versed in shared musical practices, African plantation workers were forced to channel their strong sense of rhythm in new directions. The steady beat of sledgehammer blows or hand claps provided a regular rhythmic foundation over which their sung melodies could explore simplified versions of the 'cross-rhythms' (rhythmic dislocations conflicting with the basic metre) so characteristic of the music of their homeland. Cross-rhythms employ 'syncopation' (in which a weak beat is made strong by accentuation), and this technique is to be seen in transcriptions of slave songs collected for an anthology, *Slave Songs of the United States*, published in New York in 1867. The volume includes a rowing song in which the editors noticed that the sung notes tended to lag slightly behind the regular motion of the oars, an early example of a procedure for promoting rhythmic momentum that later evolved

11

into the 'swung rhythm' of jazz. Similar use of syncopation was observed in the collections of slave songs from the Georgia Sea Islands compiled by Lydia Parrish from 1909 onwards.

Another rhythmic technique originating in African music that later exerted a widespread influence on jazz has been called 'additive rhythm' by musicologists. It works on the principle that all regular pulses may be subdivided into groups of either two or three beats, according to where the accents are placed. A group of eight beats can be subdivided equally into 2+2+2+2(=4+4), as was common in classical music before the twentieth century, or split unequally in the 'additive' patterns 3+3+2, 3+2+3 or 2+3+3. Almost all jazz brings additive patterns such as these into conflict with regular accompanying patterns to create cross-rhythms that propel the music forwards; they are especially prominent in ragtime. Additive rhythm is also a feature of many Caribbean and Latin American dances, and of some East European folk music.

African vocal music generally consists of a single line. In traditional African music the western concept of harmony is alien; it was only later, as the influence of western musical traditions spread, that the harmonic dimension of jazz grew in importance. Many plantation work songs were constructed, like their African tribal prototypes, on a 'call-and-response' pattern in which a lead voice sings an exhortation and is immediately echoed by a response from the chorus. The structure of the entire song consists of continuous alternations of solo and chorus, the leader's solo sections sometimes incorporating improvised embellishments. Improvisation later became a fundamental (many might say *the* fundamental) characteristic of jazz, and the feature that most clearly differentiates it from classical music. Much African music is based on variation procedures loosely analogous to the most common structure in jazz: successive improvised variations on a borrowed melody, each solo variation known (somewhat confusingly) as a 'chorus'. The call-and-response pattern of work songs may also have inspired certain antiphonal effects in later jazz styles: the juxtaposition of short phrases in different registers in ragtime and 'stride' piano, the alternation of short phrases for different instrumental groupings in the big-band music of the Swing Era, and the procedure known as 'trading fours', in which the members of a small ensemble play four-bar phrases in strict rotation. Similarly, the direct repetition of material in some jazz styles (as in the 'riff') may reflect African influences. Another jazz technique, in which an improvised section is terminated by a signal from the lead musician (known as 'on the nod'), has a clear

6 Tribal drummers
   from Angola,
   West Africa.

parallel in the structural control exerted by the master drummer in African tribal music, who directs the performance by means of similar spontaneous signals.

Both the tone quality and melodic style of African singing ultimately had some impact on jazz, whether sung or played. In striking contrast to the anodyne, pure tone for which classical musicians invariably strive, 'dirty' tone is not only permissible in jazz but is also considered to be expressive and characterful. The deliberate playing of notes that to western ears can seem out of tune is considered a viable device in many ethnic musics, and is another feature of jazz not to be found in classical music. The prominent sliding from one note to another in jazz melodies (known as *portamento*) may also have originated in African singing, while the expressive nonsense syllables of 'scat' singing seem to have been inspired by the sonorous nuances of African languages. It is significant, too, that jazz wind players from Louis Armstrong to John Coltrane have often tried to imitate the inflections of the human voice in their playing, since in African instrumental music the rhythmic patterns are invariably related to the inflections and stresses of the native language, and sometimes even to a specific text.

13

The tonal system of African music left its mark on jazz in the shape of the so-called 'blue note'. Some African scales are superficially similar to western examples, and to the pentatonic (five-note) scales – such as that obtained by playing the black notes of the piano – ubiquitous in almost all folk-music traditions and constituting one of the most ancient and fundamental of musical resources. The origin of blue notes may be explained in two ways. The expressive bending of pitches in African singing was retained and systematized in jazz in the form of flattened inflections of the third, fifth and seventh degrees of the western major scale. Flattened sevenths are to be found as early as the 1867 anthology of slave songs, and flattened thirds and sevenths appear regularly in early jazz (the flattened fifth becoming more prominent in the 1940s). Alternatively, blue notes may represent vestigial traces of African pentatonic scales, since the flattening of the third and seventh degrees cancels out the semitone steps that characterize the western major scale.

All these putative examples of African influence on jazz filtered their way into the new style through various black musical idioms popular in the nineteenth century. The most striking feature of these genres is the manner in which they borrow techniques from European music and adapt them in order to retain stylistic links with those quasi-African elements outlined above. In the early nineteenth century there was a general increase in the number of black musicians able to play western instruments; musical ability could even raise the value of a slave when sold from one owner to another. The violin was adopted by black musicians with widespread success, the potential for *portamento* in fiddle technique allowing its melodic idiom to be clearly related to quasi-African vocal styles. Black musicians began to assimilate the musical styles favoured by their white counterparts, and increasingly provided musical entertainment for their owners or, if they already enjoyed the benefits of freedom, their former masters. They began to learn the accompaniments to popular white dances, some of which were satirized in the process, as in the case of the cakewalk. The parody of these imitations appears to have been lost on white entertainers, however, who in turn grew fond of imitating what they saw as rather quaint black music-making. This mimicry spawned the 'minstrel show', a miscellany of comedy and song performed by white musicians with blackened faces to the accompaniment of slave instruments such as the banjo and the 'bones' (sticks or bones struck together as a percussion instrument, which may have evolved as a substitute for the drums banned on some plantations). At the time

7 Lithographic poster advertising a minstrel show in 1900, featuring Doc Quigley's 'Darkey Professors'.

minstrelsy was viewed as highly entertaining and had a large following, but today it is regarded as racially offensive. (Even so, the BBC's enormously popular *Black and White Minstrel Show* managed to survive on television until the 1970s before being deemed racist.) After the Civil War, in a development rich with irony, black musicians began to copy these white imitations of their own practices, and many of the finest early jazz singers began their careers in minstrel shows. Some Afro-American performers even felt compelled to darken their faces to emphasize their African origins, a bizarre trick that persisted in later years: Jelly Roll Morton and Billie Holiday both used black make-up at some stage in their careers because the expectation among the white audience was that jazz performers should be dark-skinned. Musically, the minstrel shows were important in fusing the syncopated manner of plantation singing with a harmonic accompaniment derived entirely from European music, even if performed on a banjo.

8 Detail from
*Negro Dancer and
Banjo Player* (1835)
by Nicolino Calyo
(1799–1884).

9 The Fisk Jubilee Singers, whose highly professional performances earned widespread critical acclaim at the end of the nineteenth century.

Pressure on black people to conform to white religious observance was another factor prompting a fusion of elements from both black and white musical practices. When black worshippers attended churches with a predominantly white congregation they learnt the simple harmonic style of European hymns, which they began to adapt to their own ends in the genre of the spiritual. This vocal music grew in importance when black communities formed their own breakaway church groups after emancipation. Retaining the harmonic idiom of Christian hymns, spirituals added the responsorial structure of work songs and were sometimes accompanied by the quasi-African 'ring shout' dance, in which the participants describe a slowly rotating circle in shuffling steps. Blue notes were included for melancholy inflections of the text, which frequently expressed the need for spiritual and physical freedom. With the rise to national prominence in the 1870s of the all-black Fisk Jubilee Singers from Nashville, Tennessee, who partly modelled their style of performance on white choirs, the spiritual became established as a respectable and distinctly American musical genre. The inexorable rhythm of plantation work songs was also emulated in black church services by the clapping accompanying communal expressions of praise; where such clapping occurred consistently on the weak off-beats, it provided a striking precursor of the heavy 'backbeats' borrowed by jazz from rock music in the 1970s.

Another genre that had a major influence on jazz at the turn of the century was the blues, in some respects a secular counterpart to the spiritual. Because blues performances are traditionally improvised and were not preserved in sound recordings until the 1920s, any account of the genre's origins must remain largely speculative, although Paul Oliver has drawn attention to the intriguing similarities, both in social position and musical technique, between blues singers and the griot musician-entertainers of those African countries that came under the influence of Islam. Initially the blues may have arisen as an amalgamation of the field holler and the work song: the solo voice comes from the former tradition and the use of call-and-response patterns recalls the latter. Originally associated with a state of deep melancholy, the blues expanded to incorporate light-hearted lyrics in a comic vein, often with a high degree of sexual innuendo. Until the late nineteenth century, as with all black musical genres, blues were probably sung unaccompanied, but the growing awareness of European music prompted the use of an accompanying harmony instrument, typically guitar or piano. The coupling of solo voice and guitar has remained a strong tradition in the singing of the so-called 'country blues', a practice that may extend as far back as the Civil War years.

In the first decade of the twentieth century, blues texts achieved a standardized form comprising three-line stanzas in which the first two lines are identical and the third rhymes with them. The vocal melody closely follows the rhythm of the text in the manner of sung speech, and tends to assume a descending contour at the end of each phrase. Each line of sung text is immediately followed by a short guitar interlude, a scheme reflecting the influence of the call-and-response patterns of African and plantation music. Blue notes, especially the flattened third and seventh, are so prominent that it is difficult to think of the blues as inhabiting either a conventional major or minor key system. The blues employs syncopation, but takes a much more flexible approach to rhythm and metre than the other genres discussed so far. Each stanza is accompanied by a simple progression of chords derived from European harmony. The specific chords used were probably selected because of the ease with which they harmonize blue notes, and the most common pattern lasts for twelve bars.

10 William Christopher Handy, posing as a teenage cornettist around 1890.

10   The blues ceased to be a strictly oral tradition when W. C. Handy (1873–1958), a bandleader from Alabama with a background in minstrelsy, published his *Memphis Blues* in 1912 in an arrangement with piano accompaniment that clearly owes much to the ragtime idiom. This and other famous blues compositions by Handy, including his *St Louis Blues* (1914), became jazz standards and exerted a strong influence on the development of the new medium. The great success in the 1920s of recordings by Mamie Smith (1883–1946), the first examples of blues to be cut by a black singer, led to the finest vaudeville artistes working closely with leading jazz musicians in recording sessions that did much to break down the distinction between blues

14   and jazz. The subtle and highly expressive phrasing of Bessie Smith (1894–1937), known as the 'Empress of the Blues', had a profound influence on later jazz singers – and, indeed, instrumentalists. Her recording of *St Louis Blues* in 1925, accompanied by Louis Armstrong on cornet and Fred Longshaw on harmonium, marks the high point of these early jazz-blues interpretations.

11 W. C. Handy's claim to originality is vaunted by this reissue of his popular *St Louis Blues*, which hails its composer as an innovator in both ragtime and jazz.

12 Mamie Smith poses with her Jazz
Hounds in New York in 1920, with Willie
'The Lion' Smith seated at the piano.

13 Meade Lux Lewis (far left), in company with fellow pianists Art Tatum, Pete Johnson and Erroll Garner.

The blues continued to exert a direct influence on jazz in the development of the 'boogie-woogie' idiom, which formed a sharp contrast to the sophisticated 'stride' piano style. Boogie-woogie adapted the twelve-bar blues progression for the keyboard in a moderate or fast tempo, using repetitive left-hand figurations often characterized by snappy dotted rhythms to prolong the simple harmonies. The harsher sounds produced when blue notes are performed on a keyboard rather than by a voice or by instruments of variable pitch (and thus capable of subtle inflections) give jazz piano playing its distinctive flavour. The boogie-woogie style reached the height of its popularity in the 1940s with new recordings of compositions such as *Honky Tonk Train Blues* (1927) by the Chicago pianist Meade Lux Lewis (1905–64), and brought renewed attention to the work of Pete Johnson (1904–67) and

14 Bessie Smith at the height of her career in 1928, shortly before she appeared in the movie *St Louis Blues*. Like many early jazz performers, she began her career in minstrelsy and vaudeville.

15 Smith recorded prolifically on the Columbia label, which launched a 'race records' series in 1923.

Albert Ammons (1907–49). Neither as refined nor as structurally inventive as the Harlem stride style, boogie-woogie was probably the legacy of an older tradition inherited from untrained black pianists and ultimately proved to be too basic an idiom to develop beyond its inherent limitations. Its distinctively repetitive style survived in the 1950s in the guise of rock and roll, which also used the twelve-bar blues progression as its harmonic foundation.

From the 1920s onwards the improvised country blues with guitar accompaniment began to grow as an independent genre. Many of its most impressive exponents were blind, and took this affliction as a title: Blind Lemon Jefferson (1897–c. 1930), a gifted Texan, recorded extensively for the Paramount label before dying in obscurity. More famous was the convicted double murderer Huddie 'Leadbelly' Ledbetter (1889–1949), who was discovered languishing in a Louisiana prison farm by John Lomax and – or so the legend goes – pardoned and released in 1934 when he sang for his prison governors.

From the blues, jazz had derived its emotional intensity, its improvisational sophistication and many of its vocal and instrumental mannerisms. Whether or not these ultimately sprang directly from African music remains open to question. Any discussion of the extent of African influence on the jazz idiom emerging at the turn of the nineteenth and twentieth centuries must remain conjectural in the absence of any sound recordings. The African influence on jazz has often been overstated for political reasons, and the substantial debt jazz owes to European musical techniques, most clearly seen in the refined idiom of ragtime, should also be acknowledged. In the hands of the most innovative musicians at the turn of the century, ragtime gradually borrowed elements from the blues to create an early form of jazz. Nevertheless, the transitional genres of black music were so important in developing American musical culture that the Czech composer Antonín Dvořák (1841–1904), in a controversial and provocative statement written for the February 1895 issue of *Harper's New Monthly Magazine*, could realistically advise American composers to build their future music on Negro melodies.

16 Blues singer Blind Lemon Jefferson around 1928.

CHAPTER TWO

Ragtime and its Influence

The ragtime idiom, which flourished between the 1890s and 1910s, is the only stylistic precursor of jazz for which any tangible evidence survives: unlike the blues, ragtime was pre-composed and could therefore be circulated in printed form. The genre derives its name from a corruption of the expression 'ragged time', referring to the ubiquitous syncopated rhythms that the genre later bequeathed to jazz. Its phenomenal, if short-lived, success was the result of the canny commercial instincts of publishers who appreciated the extent of the popular market for domestic piano music and commissioned the finest composers of light music to write within clearly defined stylistic limitations. Scott Joplin and others made strenuous attempts to promote ragtime as a new classical genre in its own right – the first in which coloured musicians had been allowed to participate actively.

Ragtime developed gradually from earlier nineteenth-century American music. Several pieces of popular salon music for solo piano by Louis Moreau Gottschalk (1829–69) were based on Latin American or slave melodies, often sporting picturesque titles such as *Bamboula, danse de nègres* (1849) or *Le Banjo (Fantaisie grotesque*; 1855). When these ethnic melodies were combined with white dance forms, as in the polka *Pasquinade* (*c.* 1860), Gottschalk's music looked directly ahead to the ragtime style. *Pasquinade* has an 'oom-pah' bass in the left hand,

17 The title page of Scott Joplin's *Maple Leaf Rag* (1899), which soon made its composer a national celebrity.

18 Louis Moreau Gottschalk as he appeared on the cover of his *Murmures éoliens* in 1862.

comprising low bass notes on the strong beats of the bar alternating with middle-register chords on the weak beats. Over this is presented a simple, catchy melody with prominent syncopations and rapid, unsubtle changes of key at the end of each section. This texture of syncopated melody and unwavering 'oom-pah' accompaniment may well have been inspired by the syncopated slave songs with banjo accompaniment performed on southern plantations. Gottschalk's compositions were well known on both sides of the Atlantic and sufficiently popular to be available via mail order in the United States; musically literate black pianists such as Joplin (who studied classical music with a German teacher in his youth) would certainly have been familiar with his work.

An orchestrated version of *Pasquinade* was in the repertoire of the celebrated concert band founded in 1892 by the 'March King', John Philip Sousa (1854–1932), which recorded it for the Victor label in 1901. Sousa's marches, which were among the most popular pieces in America in the last years of the nineteenth century, formed the other principal precursor of ragtime. Marches were composed in a number of repeated sections, the last one or two of which moved to a new key. Both the sectionalized structure and change of key were retained in ragtime, along with the basic four- or two-beat march metre. Many published rags were subtitled 'march' or carried the tempo marking 'in slow march time'. Closely related to both the march and ragtime was the cakewalk, an entertainment said to have originated among the Seminole Indians in Florida, who satirized the pomposity of white behaviour by holding dancing competitions for which a cake was awarded as a prize. Once ragtime became popular, the Sousa Band frequently performed orchestrated versions of piano rags and cake-walks; their European tours from 1900 to 1905 introduced the new style to composers such as Claude Debussy (1862–1918), who later attempted to synthesize ragtime and concert music.

One of the strictly limited employment opportunities for black musicians after emancipation was the lowly post of brothel pianist. Those who could read music were inevitably dubbed 'Professor', and were considered the élite of jobbing musicians; the rest were mere 'ticklers', who tickled the ivories. Ragtime appears to have evolved when these enterprising keyboard players adapted popular marches for performance on the honky-tonk pianos used to entertain clients in the 'sporting houses' of city red-light districts. Almost all ragtime and early jazz pianists gained their early performing experience in this context, and it was to be many decades before the music's association with immoral pursuits could be shaken off. Some, such as Jelly Roll Morton, combined their musical responsibilities with pimping, since playing the piano was a convenient way of maintaining a close watch on the establishment's professional activities. An impressive concentration of early jazz talent was nurtured in the legalized red-light district at Storyville in New Orleans.

Early ragtime was undoubtedly improvised, but in 1895 songs in ragtime style appeared in print for the first time. They often sported racist titles that are unacceptable today, such as *All Coons Look Alike to Me* by Ernest Hogan (who, amazingly, was himself black). The first instrumental rag, *Mississippi Rag* by William H. Krell, was published in 1897. It was ironic that the first piano rag to appear in print was written by a white composer and that the first jazz recordings twenty years later were cut by a white group. Both events reflected the comparative ease with which Caucasians could achieve commercial success. The first piano rag to be published by a black musician was Tom Turpin's *Harlem Rag*, issued nearly a year after Krell's piece. Many rags, whether by black or white composers, promoted racial stereotypes of black Americans in their cover artwork and titles. Some were deemed sufficiently offensive in 1973, when reproduced in an important anthology of ragtime, to warrant a special note from the American publishers commenting on 'the broader humor of their era, in which the nation was far less sensitive to jibes about minority groups. It is our belief that a mature understanding of our past is more fruitful than a falsification of history'.

19 Tom Turpin, the first black composer to publish an instrumental rag, composed his *St Louis Rag* in 1903.

20 Scott Joplin was the first black composer to experience the tension between commercial viability and high artistic aspirations.

Tom Turpin became well known after 1900 as the proprietor of the Rosebud Café in St Louis, Missouri, which established itself as a meeting place for many itinerant pianists. Among his associates was Scott Joplin (1868–1917), the son of a railway worker, who had appeared as a pianist at the Chicago World's Fair in 1893. Joplin settled in Sedalia, Missouri, where he enrolled at the George R. Smith Negro College to further his musical education. This may not have proved to be an entirely congenial environment, however: on 14 April 1905 the college's newsletter issued a *caveat* against treating music associated with bordellos too seriously. In Sedalia, Joplin played at a gambling den before taking up the post of pianist at the Maple Leaf Club, which gave its name to Joplin's *Maple Leaf Rag*. The work was published in 1899 by John Stark, who bought it for only $50 and saw it sell 75,000 copies in just six months. By the time of Joplin's death, sales of *Maple Leaf Rag* had exceeded one million copies.

17

Joplin's perennially popular piece is typical of the ragtime style as it evolved in the Midwest. It clearly owes its metre and tempo marking ('Tempo di marcia'), western harmonic idiom and sectionalized structure to the march. In *Maple Leaf Rag* the highly syncopated melody includes a number of figurations recalling banjo techniques, which Joplin may have learnt from his mother (who played the instrument); the title page of his first published rag, entitled *Original Rags* (1898), carried the legend 'picked by Scott Joplin' – a phrase associated with plucking the banjo. Many of the syncopations involve subdividing eight pulse units into the additive pattern 3+3+2 to create cross-rhythms against the regular bass part in the left hand, a feature ultimately derived from African and Latin American music.

21 The opening section of Joplin's *Maple Leaf Rag.*

22 Joseph Lamb's *Ethiopia*, a rag published by John Stark in 1909, featured a stereotypical African scene on its cover.

23 Joseph Lamb in 1915. His work reinforced the strong links between the ragtime style and earlier salon music by white composers.

In places Joplin's style recalls techniques of nineteenth-century black folk music. In addition to the prominent use of syncopation and imitations of banjo figurations, he occasionally emulates call-and-response patterns, as in the contrasted high and low phrases juxtaposed in the opening theme of the ragtime two-step *The Entertainer* (1902). In fact, the ragtime style epitomized by Joplin's work owed far more to white traditions than to African practices, as Joachim Berendt emphasized in his epigrammatic description of the genre as 'white music – played black'.

Flush from the phenomenal success of *Maple Leaf Rag*, Stark and Joplin moved east to St Louis and set up the so-called 'Missouri School' of 'classic' ragtime. Stark's publishing company also promoted the music of two younger talents: the black composer James Scott (1886–1918) and the white composer Joseph Lamb (1887–1962). Lamb's work in particular is marked by a sensitive lyricism, his unusual minor-key *Ragtime Nightingale* (1915) seeming to echo the piano music of Chopin and Liszt, which had originally influenced Gottschalk's salon pieces.

Joplin produced a slow but steady stream of high-quality ragtime pieces after 1900, creating about thirty in all. He also adapted rag characteristics to other dance forms, such as the waltz. Stark's relationship

33

24 Stark's shortened version of Joplin's *The Ragtime Dance* appeared as 'A Stop-Time Two Step' in 1906.

with Joplin began to deteriorate when Joplin started to embark on more ambitious compositional projects with limited commercial potential. First came a ragtime ballet, *The Ragtime Dance*, which occupied him between 1899 and 1902. Stark only agreed to publish it in a severely truncated form. Next Joplin devoted his energies to an operatic project under the title *A Guest of Honor*, written around 1903 and now lost. He moved to New York in 1907 and began to channel his energies into another opera, *Treemonisha*. Published at his own expense in 1911 and performed privately in Harlem four years later, the work had little artistic merit, being written in a bland classical idiom at least fifty years out of date and setting an uninspired libretto concerning the desired progression of black people from their world of superstition and ritual to the true enlightenment of education. Not surprisingly, the 1915 performance was not a critical success. Bitterly disillusioned, Joplin died in 1917 after a nervous breakdown.

It was in the year of Joplin's death that the new jazz craze spectacularly began to flourish with the success of the first recordings by the Original Dixieland Jazz Band. Although they had provided a

34

firm foundation for the early jazz style, rags of the classic Missouri School were all but forgotten after Stark's company went out of business in 1922. The ragtime idiom became so old-fashioned that during the 1920s it would only be adopted by cinema organists and pianists in order to evoke a mood of nostalgia.

Between 1908 and 1920 several distinguished European composers were influenced by ragtime, initially inspired by performances of the touring Sousa Band. Oddly, most American classical composers do not seem to have been attracted to the idiom at this stage: a rare exception is encountered in a piano sonata written around 1909 by the New England insurance salesman and amateur avant-garde composer Charles Ives (1874–1954), which distorts ragtime features in an eccentric manner typical of its composer. In Europe, ragtime was seized upon as a style that owed nothing to the post-Wagnerian idiom of late romantic music against which many composers were then beginning to rebel. Debussy, who probably heard the Sousa Band at the Paris Exposition in 1900, emulated Joplin's style in his 'Golliwog's Cakewalk' from the *Children's Corner* suite (1908) and wickedly included a quotation from Wagner's opera *Tristan und Isolde*. Debussy again adopted rag characteristics in three later piano pieces: *Le petit nègre* (1909) and the preludes 'Minstrels' (1910) and 'General Lavine: excentric [sic]' (1913). In 1917, Erik Satie (1866–1925) incorporated in his ballet *Parade* references to a ragtime song by Irving Berlin, whose *Alexander's Ragtime Band* (composed in 1911) had done much to popularize a diluted version of the idiom. The culmination of this trend is to be seen in the work of Igor Stravinsky (1882–1971), who composed a series of rag-inspired works in which elements of the style

25 The three composers working in France who flirted with ragtime are all represented by this image: Debussy (left), Stravinsky (right) and Satie (who took the photograph at Debussy's Paris home in 1910).

are subjected to an ingenious process of distortion. The first of these experiments is to be found in the ragtime dance in *The Soldier's Tale* (1918), which was followed by the solo piano piece *Piano-Rag-Music* (written for Artur Rubinstein in 1919) and *Ragtime for Eleven Instruments* (also 1919). In the last, a gypsy cimbalom (a form of dulcimer) is made to sound uncannily like the clattering of a honky-tonk piano.

In the ragtime era, recording was carried out by the 'acoustic' process. Musicians played into a large horn through which the vibrations were transmitted directly to a cutting needle in contact with a rotating master disc made from soft wax. This primitive technology was far from satisfactory, and most pianists preferred to record their interpretations of ragtime pieces by cutting rolls for the highly popular player-pianos (pianolas). Scott Joplin's performances at the keyboard were only preserved for posterity in this medium. Piano rolls are generally unreliable as an authentic record of live performance, however, because technicians sometimes made additions, resulting in rich textures unplayable with just two hands. In extreme cases, the entire 'performance' might be fabricated in a workshop without a single finger coming into contact with a keyboard. Once the jangly, exciting noise generated by piano rolls became popular, the speed of ragtime inevitably increased, and its melodic figurations became more virtuosic, especially in the work of composers based on the East Coast. A good example of this brilliant 'novelty' style is George Botsford's *Black and White Rag* (1908), which achieved renewed popularity in Britain during the 1970s when the BBC chose it as the signature tune for its snooker programme *Pot Black*. In 1908 Joplin published his *School of Ragtime*, six exercises for piano with a verbal introduction aiming to restore a restrained manner of performance. The ragtime pianist was warned: 'We wish to say here that the "Joplin ragtime" is destroyed by careless or imperfect rendering, and very often good players lose the effect entirely, by playing too fast. They are harmonized with the supposition that each note will be played as it is written, as it takes this, and also the proper time divisions, to complete the sense intended.' Many of Joplin's printed scores began to carry at the top of their first page the instruction: 'Notice! Don't play this piece fast. It is never right to play "Ragtime" fast.'

26 The cover design to Stravinsky's *Ragtime for Eleven Instruments* (1919), a depiction of a violinist and banjo player drawn in a single uninterrupted line by Pablo Picasso.

Igor Strawinsky
RAGTIME

ÉDITIONS DE LA Sirene - 12 R. LA BOËTIE - PARIS

Joplin was fighting a losing battle, for it had become increasingly common for pianists to add their own embellishments to existing rag compositions. As part of a recorded retrospective made for the Library of Congress in 1938, Jelly Roll Morton reconstructed his manner of playing *Maple Leaf Rag* in the first decade of the century. The syncopations have become jazzier, and rhythmic dislocations formerly confined to the right hand are now inserted in the left-hand part to destroy the complacently unwavering 'oom-pah' pattern. Joplin's harmonies are recognizable beneath the decoration, and provide the structural foundation for Morton's embellishments. Morton declared in his memoirs: 'Ragtime is a certain type of syncopation and only certain tunes can be played in that idea. But jazz is a style that can be applied to any type of tune. I started using the word in 1902 to show people the difference between jazz and ragtime.' The date Morton gives may stretch credibility to the limit (he was only twelve in 1902), but 'jazzing up' had evidently become widespread and was not confined to ragtime: Morton lavished the same treatment on popular classics, such as arias from Verdi's operas. When James Scott wrote his pointedly titled *Don't Jazz Me Rag – I'm Music* in 1921, it was far too late to reverse the trend.

27 A selection of representative piano recordings made for the Blue Note label between 1939 and 1945 was issued on CD in 1992.

The more exciting, jazzed-up ragtime idiom developed directly into the first recognizable keyboard style in jazz: that of the Harlem 'stride' school, which was nurtured in New York's black enclave. This music was featured at the so-called 'rent parties' given by impoverished tenants to raise the money for their rent. Paying guests were invited to musical gatherings with 'cutting contests', in which one pianist tried to outplay another. The stride style took its name from the striding motion of the left hand, which now alternated bass notes and off-beat chords with far greater rapidity and heaviness than in earlier ragtime. The left-hand chords tended to contain more notes and explored more advanced harmonies; over them, the right-hand figurations were supple, inventive and frequently virtuosic, without sacrificing expressiveness and melodic charm. Stride compositions often retained the sectionalized, multi-thematic structure of ragtime as well as its metre. The addition of blue notes, which had slowly begun to appear in some piano rags, imbued the style with a jazzier flavour; the twelve-bar blues progression had also influenced earlier ragtime pieces, and now left its mark on the stride and boogie-woogie piano styles. Improvised embellishments were now rife; their flexibility was particularly apparent when performers recorded the same piece on different occasions.

Another new tendency was 'swung' rhythm, which became commonplace in later jazz. It consisted of two techniques: alternating notes of long and short time values to produce a lilting effect, and playing accented notes or chords slightly in advance of the main beats. As in Morton's demonstration of jazzed-up ragtime, far more melodic interest and rhythmic complexity were permitted in the left hand than had been the case in earlier rags. Irregular patterns such as the 3+3+2 additive rhythm now disrupted the formerly staid and regular bass part to add excitement.

All jazz pianists in the 1920s grew up with the Harlem style as their basic musical language, but the left-hand patterns required such technical skill that only the ablest could become truly proficient. Some of the best failed to achieve the fame they deserved: one example was Steve Lewis, pianist with Armand Piron's band in New York, who in 1923 cut a spirited piano roll of *Mama's Gone, Goodbye*. Others, like George Gershwin, have been better served by posterity, although Gershwin's considerable skill as a stride pianist has always been overshadowed by his formidable reputation as a composer. 28

The greatest exponent of the Harlem idiom was undoubtedly James P. Johnson (1894–1955), who earned himself the nickname 'Father 29

28 Armand Piron's orchestra in 1924, with Steve Lewis at the piano.

of Stride Piano'. It was his *Charleston* – with its particularly clear examples of the rhythmic anticipations mentioned above – that defined for many the infectious gaiety of the early jazz epoch. The *Charleston*, named after the town in South Carolina from which many of the New York stevedores hailed, was included in Johnson's Broadway show, *Runnin' Wild*, which enjoyed great success in 1923 when it ran for no fewer than 213 performances.

In company with many New York pianists, Johnson had a thorough grounding in European classical music, made a point of dressing elegantly and habitually played with a cigar held in his clenched teeth – a trademark of several of the finest stride pianists, among whom the cult of the jazz personality first began to assert itself. Initially influenced by the ragtime pianist Eubie Blake (1883–1983), whose work typified the more virtuosic Eastern rag style centred on Baltimore, Johnson's endlessly resourceful exploration of the Harlem idiom is best shown by his effervescent *Carolina Shout*. Composed around 1917 and recorded by

30

29 James P. Johnson, 'Father of Stride Piano', around 1945.

its composer live four years later, the piece was inspired by the call-and-response patterns of the ring shout, which are directly emulated in some of the musical phrasing. Unlike ragtime pieces, *Carolina Shout* is based on a single chord progression and is therefore closer to later jazz structures. It was from this masterpiece of the stride school, which sounds fresh even today, that the young Duke Ellington learnt his early piano style, slowing down the version for piano roll that Johnson had made in 1918 so that he could memorize the patterns reproduced by the pianola keys. Ellington was also influenced by the stride pianist Willie 'The Lion' Smith (1897–1973), whose compositions owed a debt to Debussy and sported impressionistic titles such as *Echoes of Spring* and *Rippling Waters*. Smith recalled having learnt blues characteristics from the published compositions of W. C. Handy, whereas Johnson claimed to have picked them up directly from the Carolina stevedores – a further illustration of the dangers inherent in overstating the African influence on early jazz styles.

Ellington was just one of many later pianists on whom Johnson made a profound impression. It was thanks to the popularity of Johnson's gifted protégé, Thomas 'Fats' Waller (1904–43), that the stride style continued to flourish in the 1930s and 1940s. Like Ellington, Waller originally learnt to mimic Johnson's playing by studying the piano roll of *Carolina Shout*, which he later recorded himself. He became proficient as a cinema organist, working at the Lincoln Theater in New York, where he received advice from the young American bandleader and composer Count Basie. (In later years, Waller shocked the musical establishment by improvising on

30 Ragtime pianist Eubie Blake (left)
with singer and lyricist Noble Sissle at the
Paramount Theater, St Louis, in 1925.

31 Fats Waller (right) records with
The Deep River Boys at RCA
Victor's New York studios in 1942.

32 James Reese Europe (far left) at sea with the band of the 369th US Infantry Regiment, 'The Hellfighters', which he took on tour to Europe in February 1918.

the organ at the cathedral of Notre-Dame in Paris.) Waller's slick technique and comic manner combined to make him one of the most popular jazz performers of all time. His songs to lyrics by Andy Razaf, including such classics as *Ain't Misbehavin'* and *Honeysuckle Rose*, were immortalized in numerous recordings with his group Fats Waller and his Rhythm. Although his solo-piano compositions in the Johnson style, some with titles like *Handful of Keys* and *Smashing Thirds* that graphically suggest the music's virtuosity and brilliance, are highly memorable, they rarely attain the degree of structural sophistication achieved by his less flamboyant mentor. After Waller, stride textures and rhythmic patterns continued to influence a later generation of jazz pianists, including Art Tatum, Thelonious Monk and Oscar Peterson.

44

Classic Missouri ragtime has enjoyed two revivals since it was eclipsed by jazz in the 1920s. The first took place in the late 1940s as part of a growing awareness of the history of jazz, which, since Benny Goodman's legendary concert at Carnegie Hall in 1938, had found new respectability and was regarded as worthy of scholarly attention. Various attempts were made to re-create the sound of early ragtime orchestras, such as the black American military band 'The Hellfighters' conducted by James Reese Europe during World War I. The second revival was largely prompted by the phenomenal success at the box office of the motion picture *The Sting* (1973), which used Joplin's *The Entertainer* as its main title theme and other Joplin pieces, including *Pineapple Rag*, as incidental music; an anachronistic application, as it happens, since the film is set in 1936. The movie won seven Oscars, and demand for Joplin's rags became so high that the sheet music of *The Entertainer*, which shot to the top of the pop charts, was once again to be found in most music shops. The 1970s also saw the emergence of a restrained and austere manner of performing ragtime, promoted by the pianist Joshua Rifkin (b. 1944), of which Joplin would undoubtedly have approved. In the wake of this resurgence of interest in Joplin's work, America's first internationally famous black composer was posthumously awarded a Pulitzer prize in 1976 for his opera *Treemonisha*, which had been revived in Atlanta in 1972 and was at last recorded by Deutsche Grammophon in 1975.

33 Scott Joplin's opera *Treemonisha*, seen here in its flamboyant production at Houston Grand Opera in 1975, which was recorded by Deutsche Grammophon. The work's failure to gain recognition in 1915 precipitated the composer's early death in 1917.

CHAPTER THREE

From New Orleans to Chicago

New Orleans has traditionally been viewed as the cradle of jazz, not only by scholars but also by many of the performers who were nurtured there, musicians of the stature of Louis Armstrong, Jelly Roll Morton and Sidney Bechet. Prosperous as a result of its commanding position at the centre of the cotton trade, with easy access to the sea and the Mississippi River, the city was a melting pot of immigrants from Africa, Britain, France, Germany and Spain. At the end of the nineteenth century, as freed slaves gradually became concentrated in city ghettoes, a quarter of the inhabitants of New Orleans were black; and this significant minority enjoyed greater freedom and opportunities than comparable groups in many other American cities. The situation rapidly deteriorated, however, after a controversial ruling in 1894 that the Creole population (those of mixed European and black ancestry) was to be classified as 'black'. Civil unrest followed, culminating in the appalling riots of 1900.

The city was distinguished by a preponderance of classical music (including opera), some of it performed by black ensembles, and by strong traditions of music-making among the minority groups. In terms of the subsequent evolution of jazz, however, the most important instrumental ensemble in the black society of New Orleans was the marching band, which constituted one of the few reliable sources of paid employment for black musicians. A typical instrumentation, as exemplified by the famous Onward Brass Band (which originally flourished between the 1880s and 1930 and was reformed in 1960), comprised three cornets or trumpets, two trombones, two clarinets or saxophones, euphonium, tuba and limited percussion (snare drum and combined bass drum/cymbal). The proliferation of bands appears to have been stimulated by the wide availability of cheap second-hand brass instruments discarded by military bands after the Civil War and the Spanish-American War (1898).

34 The Onward Brass Band in New Orleans around 1913, with leader Manuel Perez on the far left.

The marching bands of New Orleans performed at many outdoor functions, including the often lavish funerals organized by burial societies within the black community. A prominent feature of processions to and from the burial ground was the inaccurately named 'second line', armed with a variety of improvised weapons, which in fact marched in front and had the task of protecting the mourners from attacks by rival gangs at the boundaries between neighbouring districts. Solemn music accompanied the mourners on the way to the cemetery. In celebration of the deceased's life, spirited music with characteristics of ragtime – an idiom derived from band marches in the first place – was played during the return from the graveyard and at the all-night wake that followed.

The novel syncopated style might be applied to classical pieces such as Chopin's famous Funeral March (from his B flat minor piano sonata), an early example of the 'jazzing up' of the classics that would later fall into disrepute. Recordings of marching bands are rare; the earliest date from 1945, by which time the influence of jazz had undoubtedly transformed the original style. Some of its crude vigour was captured during the New Orleans funeral scene in the James Bond movie *Live and Let Die* (1973) with the energetic playing of Harold 'Duke' Dejan's Olympia Brass Band, a group founded in the city in 1958.

35 Buddy Bolden (back row, second from right) and his band, *c.* 1895.

36, 37 (opposite) Bunk Johnson (fourth from left) and his New Orleans band around 1947, with guest singer Connie Boswell (seated).

Many jazz musicians served their apprenticeships in the New Orleans marching bands, which determined the choice of the trumpet, trombone and clarinet as the principal melodic instruments in early jazz. The first jazz trumpeter of note was Charles 'Buddy' Bolden (1877–1931), who led his own band from the 1890s until 1907, when he was abruptly interred in a lunatic asylum (for hitting his mother-in-law over the head) before having the opportunity to make any recordings. As a result, is impossible to be certain about his style of playing, although his fellow trumpeter Bunk Johnson (1889–1949) attempted to reconstruct it during the 1940s revival of early jazz. The instrumentation of Bolden's band established the format for most early jazz ensembles in its combination of three melody instruments (trumpet or cornet, clarinet and trombone) and a supporting 'rhythm section' (guitar, doublebass and drums).

49

Bolden preferred – as did Louis Armstrong in his early years – the mellower tone of the cornet to that of the trumpet, and it seems likely that the strong European presence in New Orleans was responsible for the vogue enjoyed by the instrument. Creole musicians based in the downtown 'Frenchtown' district, such as the Onward Brass Band's lead cornettist Manuel Perez (1871–1946), were musically literate, and cultivated a refined form of dance music based on ragtime. Bolden is acknowledged to have been the first performer to integrate the sectionalized structures and harmonic practices of Creole dance music with the less refined but more spontaneous and emotionally powerful elements of the blues, which up to this time had been exclusively the province of the uptown black musicians. His manner of playing was influenced by the pitch-bending and expressive tone of blues singers, and in these respects he contributed to the instrumentalization of the vocal blues then becoming popular in black quarters. He was also reported to be the first musician to promote a sense of rhythmic 'swing'.

34

Bolden's group performed in New Orleans's red-light district, known as Storyville or the 'Tenderloin', which was situated close to the railway on Basin Street. It had been a centre of legalized prostitution since 1857 and serviced the needs of sailors from the nearby US naval base; in 1897 the legislation governing the district's activities was clarified by Alderman Joseph Story, who (doubtless to his subsequent chagrin) unwittingly donated his name to the region. A guide to the district's facilities, known as *The Blue Book*, contained details of the so-called 'sporting houses', including the lavishly decorated mansion run by Lulu White. Many musicians supplemented their income by playing in the district's establishments, and Storyville became a flourishing centre for southern ragtime pianists. In 1917, however, the region was closed for good in response to pressure from the US Navy and musicians were forced to seek work elsewhere. As part of an already established trend caused by widespread unemployment and economic depression in the South, they gradually migrated northwards to Chicago and New York.

It was in February 1917 that a group of white musicians from New Orleans, well known for their performances in Chicago during the previous year, made the first jazz phonograph recordings in New York. The novelty of these recordings catapulted the group to international stardom (they appeared in London in 1919), but their work was only a crude and probably outdated imitation of the black music-making then prevalent in their home city, and it remains an unfortunate irony

38 Tom Anderson's 'Arlington Annexe' in Storyville, New Orleans, with Lulu White's Mahogany Hall in the background.

that a white group should have gained such instant commercial success by unashamedly borrowing a black musical genre. Under the leadership of cornettist Nick LaRocca (1889–1961), the Original Dixieland Jazz Band was also responsible for promoting the word 'jazz' to describe their raw, earthy music. The spelling was said to have been altered from the original 'jass' because pranksters deleted the letter 'j' from the band's posters. In fact, the word 'jass' originally derived from 'orgasm' (colloquially termed 'jasm') and was an expletive. The group's first recording, *Livery Stable Blues*, became a hit, largely on account of its novelty instrumental imitations of farmyard noises. Much of the Original Dixieland Jazz Band's work is rhythmically stilted (a fundamental fault described as 'corny' by later musicians) and lacks the prominent blue notes of early black jazz.

39 The Original Dixieland Jazz Band on stage at the Hammersmith Palais
de Danse, London, in 1919. Their hats spell the word 'Dixie'.

The term 'Dixieland' is generally reserved for the New Orleans
style as adapted by white musicians. Apart from the Original Dixieland
Jazz Band, another successful white group was the New Orleans
Rhythm Kings, who were active in Chicago in the early 1920s. Both
bands modelled their instrumentation on the smaller black New
Orleans ensembles, with a three-instrument 'front line' (cornet,
clarinet and trombone), and a supporting rhythm section (including
piano and drums). The phenomenal success of these early bands was
linked to the rapid expansion of dancing stimulated by the energetic
pleasure-seeking of the younger generation. The popularity of new
dance styles helped jazz to develop from the march-like tread of its
early days into the snappy, syncopated music so characteristic of what
F. Scott Fitzgerald dubbed 'The Jazz Age'.

The first black jazz cornettist to make successful recordings in the post-Bolden style was Joe 'King' Oliver (1885–1938), whose career also began in the New Orleans brass bands and at Storyville. After World War I he joined the migration northwards and found work in Chicago, where he formed his Creole Jazz Band. The group gave fine performances at the city's Lincoln Gardens in 1922, and in April 1923 began a series of celebrated recordings in the Gennett Studios at Richmond, Indiana, which represent an early high point of the New Orleans style. The group comprised the typical front line plus a rhythm section of varying composition: it might include banjo, guitar or piano for harmonic support, with tuba or doublebass for the bass line, and drums as an optional extra. (Early recordings are unreliable documents, because primitive recording techniques often restricted the drummer to a single woodblock so that he would not drown out the rest of the ensemble, and a banjo might replace a heavy bass line to prevent the record needle from jumping.) Oliver brought together an impressive group of musicians: the four-strong front-line included Louis Armstrong on second cornet and Johnny Dodds (1892–1940) on clarinet, while his brother Baby Dodds (1898–1959) on drums was part of the rhythm section.

40 King Oliver's Creole Jazz Band in Chicago, 1923. Left to right: Baby Dodds, Honoré Dutrey, Joe Oliver, Louis Armstrong, Bill Johnson, Johnny Dodds and Lil Armstrong.

Oliver's Creole Jazz Band perfected a style of New Orleans jazz in which the three (or four) front-line instruments participated in a polyphonic elaboration of the basic melody. The cornet played the version closest to the original theme, while the more agile clarinet added decorative embellishments and the trombone provided a generally slower countermelody. Solo passages were sometimes lengthy – Oliver's famous and much-imitated solo in *Dippermouth Blues* ran to three full choruses – but appear to have been largely prepared in advance: improvisation was reserved for the two-bar unaccompanied 'breaks' that were sometimes interspersed between sections, and may also have been carefully rehearsed. Pieces either borrowed the sectionalized format of ragtime or were based on the twelve-bar blues, which now became a staple harmonic progression.

Oliver's band was distinguished by skilfully balanced and disciplined ensemble playing, and his cornet playing broke new ground in exploring the expressive possibilities of various forms of mute. However, he was unable – or unwilling – to develop the New Orleans style beyond its inherent limitations. In 1924, the Dodds brothers left the band when they discovered that Oliver had been pocketing a proportion of their earnings, and Armstrong soon followed suit. Three years later, Oliver formed a new band in New York, but he had already been eclipsed by Armstrong's technical and improvisational brilliance. In comparison with the new swing-band style of the early 1930s, Oliver's music seemed old-fashioned and was ignored. He died in 1938 while working as a janitor in a Savannah poolroom, the first casualty of the abruptly changing musical fashions so characteristic of jazz.

Another significant figure in the New Orleans style was the trombonist Kid Ory (1886–1973), who was responsible for making the first recordings by a black jazz band, in Los Angeles in 1922. Ory specialized in the 'tailgate' style – which owed its name to the custom of playing jazz on the back of an open truck – characterized by vibrant glissandos and strong rhythmic momentum.

The clarinet was promoted as a versatile jazz instrument by Johnny Dodds and several other New Orleans performers, including Jimmie Noone (1895–1944) and Sidney Bechet (1897–1959). All three also adapted clarinet technique to the demands of the saxophone, an instrument featured in early recordings as something of a novelty but soon to become the most distinctive sonority in jazz.

Bechet travelled extensively in his early years before settling temporarily in Chicago to play with King Oliver and fellow cornettist Freddie Keppard (1890–1933). In 1919, Will Marion Cook, composer

41 Sidney Bechet performs on soprano saxophone in a typical Paris cellar bar in 1949.

of the successful Broadway revue *Clorindy or The Origin of the Cakewalk* (1898), invited Bechet to join his Southern Syncopated Orchestra on a tour of Europe. The Swiss conductor Ernest Ansermet, who had heard Bechet playing in London, lavished praise on him in a published review and recommended the music of 'this artist of genius' to his friend Stravinsky. It was in London that Bechet acquired a soprano saxophone, and he became the first notable soloist on this neglected instrument. Much of his subsequent career was spent in Europe, where he developed an idiosyncratic style of playing that set him apart from his New Orleans contemporaries. Among his more bizarre musical escapades was an early experiment in overdubbing to produce a one-man-band effect in 1941. His recordings with Armstrong nevertheless demonstrate his deep affinity with the New Orleans brand of clarinet and saxophone playing.

55

42 A dapper Jelly Roll Morton poses at the piano in Chicago in 1924.

43 Morton's *Jelly Roll Blues* (1915), depicted here in a later instrumental version.

It was a New Orleans Creole pianist who did most to further the development of jazz as a music capable of sustaining structural – and hence intellectual – interest. Ferdinand 'Jelly Roll' Morton (1890–1941) was, in addition to being a talented pianist, a flamboyant entrepreneur whose exploits became (largely through self-promotion) legendary. He claimed to have created jazz single-handedly in 1902 when he began 'jazzing up' his performances and departing from the restraints of classic ragtime. In his youth he performed in Storyville, where he was a protégé of 'Professor' Tony Jackson. From 1904, when his grandmother discovered his place of work and threw him out of the family home, he branched out and began touring other cities. He maintained that he had composed his popular *Jelly Roll Blues* as early as 1905, although it was not published until 1915, when it became the first jazz work to appear in print and helped to bring the jazz style to the notice of musicians outside New Orleans. In 1922 he settled in Chicago and began recording in the following year, his output including some sides with the New Orleans Rhythm Kings in an early example of mixed-race collaboration.

In the recordings made by his own band, The Red Hot Peppers (formed in 1926), Morton conducted bold experiments with musical structures. Two important attributes made these innovations possible. First, he was a composer (not merely an interpreter of music written by others) and therefore he took a keen interest in the intellectual nature of jazz and wanted to promote it as an art form. Secondly, he was a skilled businessman and publicist who ran his band with a professionalism that was new to the jazz world. His sidemen earned fixed fees of $5 per rehearsal and $15 per recording session; rehearsals were performed with great attention to detail and Morton would stop at nothing to secure the musical effects he desired (even, on one memorable occasion, threatening a recalcitrant trombonist at gunpoint until his interpretation was acceptable). He was fortunate in having his work promoted by the white Melrose brothers, whose small but energetic Chicago publishing company took the unusually generous step of funding the band's rehearsals.

Morton was proficient as both pianist and arranger, as the solo-piano and full-ensemble recordings of his 1926 composition *The Pearls* vividly demonstrate. The Red Hot Peppers consisted of the standard New Orleans instrumentation (its members included well-known New Orleans players such as Kid Ory and Baby Dodds), and used the same polyphonic elaboration of the basic melody. Because of Morton's special talents, the piano was promoted from mere rhythm-section support to front-line solo status. The composer's solo-piano passages were firmly rooted in the post-ragtime stride style. *Black Bottom Stomp*, recorded in 1926, borrowed the sectionalized structure of ragtime but enlivened it by incorporating seemingly improvised (but probably rehearsed) solo sections and well-timed breaks for various instruments. A leading jazz scholar, Gunther Schuller, has praised Morton's compositions for managing to create 'a maximum variety of texture and timbre without sacrificing clarity of form', an achievement all the more remarkable given the essentially limited idiom within which Morton worked. The jazz historian James Lincoln Collier summed up Morton's contribution: 'He worked with only a few basic colours, and the effect was of Matisse.'

Some of Morton's pieces hark back to the days of New Orleans funeral processions: *Dead Man Blues*, which was recorded in September 1926, drew its inspiration from a genuine funeral piece called 'Flee as a Bird'. Other compositions, such as *Doctor Jazz*, look forward to later jazz in being based on a single repeating set of harmonies in contrast to the multiple sections of ragtime structures.

44 Morton (at the piano) and his Red Hot Peppers in Chicago in 1926. On the left is pioneering trombonist Kid Ory.

Recorded on 16 December 1926, *Doctor Jazz* also provides a good example of Morton's flamboyant style of singing.

Morton was an accomplished blues singer and declared that he had invented wordless 'scat' singing in 1907. Keen to promote himself as the person solely responsible for the early development of jazz, he was outraged when, in 1938, he heard radio compere Robert Ripley describe W. C. Handy as the originator of jazz and the blues. Morton sent a vitriolic letter to Ripley, with a copy to *Down Beat* magazine, and declared:

> In your broadcast of March 26, 1938, you introduced W. C.
> Handy as the originator of *jazz, stomps*, and *blues*. By this
> announcement you have done me a great injustice...
>
> It is evidently known, beyond contradiction, that New
> Orleans is the cradle of jazz, and I, myself, happened to be the
> creator in the year 1902... I met Handy in Memphis [in
> 1908]... Of course, Handy could not play any of these types
> and I can assure you has not learned them yet.
>
> ... I do not claim any of the creation of the blues, although
> I have written many of them even before Mr Handy had any
> blues published.

Never one to be troubled by false modesty, Morton had his visiting cards printed with legends such as 'Originator of Jazz-Stomp-Swing' and 'World's Greatest Hot Tune Writer'. According to jazz critic George Hoefer, Morton declared in 1940: 'New Orleans style, Chicago style, Kansas City style, New York style, IT'S ALL JELLY ROLL STYLE.'

Morton certainly deserves credit for being one of the first musicians to incorporate Latin elements in jazz (which he termed the 'Spanish tinge'). Furthermore, his duet recording of *Wolverine Blues* with clarinettist Voltaire de Faut in 1925 demonstrated that he was capable of spontaneous improvisation as well as sophisticated pre-composition.

Unfortunately for the likes of Morton and Oliver, and for New Orleans jazz in general, fashions were changing so rapidly in the late 1920s that these early masterpieces were soon forgotten. The rise of the larger swing band, with its colourful instrumentation, melodic appeal and more sophisticated harmonies, was well under way when Morton moved to New York in 1928. The polyphonic basis of the New Orleans ensembles did not lend itself easily to the new style, for the simple reason that if more than two players improvise simultaneously on anything other than a simple set of harmonies, the results are likely to be chaotic. Morton attempted to adopt some of the characteristics of the swing-band style when he founded his own big band in 1929, but his recordings with this group were unsuccessful. His composition *King Porter Stomp*, however, did find popular appeal in 1935, when it was interpreted by Benny Goodman and his swing band.

Unlike Oliver, Morton was rescued from retirement in 1938 by Alan Lomax, who had read the composer's self-publicizing letter to Robert Ripley. Lomax encouraged Morton to make a series of retrospective recordings for the Library of Congress in Washington, DC, that constitute a unique oral history of the early jazz era. Of these and the Victor recording sessions that followed, perhaps the most remarkable are his jazzed-up rendering of Joplin's *Maple Leaf Rag* and the intense and highly musical blues singing of *Whinin' Boy Blues*. Morton's untimely death in 1941 cheated him of the celebrity status he would undoubtedly have enjoyed during the revival of New Orleans jazz in the late 1940s.

45 Jelly Roll Morton's *King Porter Stomp* became a hit in the Swing Era in its energetic arrangement by Fletcher Henderson.

KING PORTER STOMP

CHAPTER FOUR

The Virtuoso: Louis Armstrong

The gradual migration of musicians northwards to Chicago after World War I was symbolized by the passage of the paddle steamers made famous by the writings of Mark Twain. These showboats plied the Mississippi from New Orleans to St Louis, where the river joined its chief tributary, the Missouri, before continuing northwards and bypassing Chicago on its western side. Steamboat companies provided a valued source of employment for black musicians each year during the summer months, when dance music was needed in the vessels' ballrooms. The most celebrated of the steamboat musicians was pianist Fate Marable (1890–1947), whose Kentucky Jazz Band worked on boats owned by the Streckfus Line in St Louis but included several prominent New Orleans musicians among its personnel. The band was sufficiently respected to be dubbed 'the floating conservatoire' by musicians, and its membership at various times included figures of the stature of Baby Dodds, Jimmy Blanton and Johnny St Cyr.

46 Louis Armstrong (second from right) with members of Fate Marable's band on the steamboat S. S. *Capitol*, operating out of St Louis in 1919.

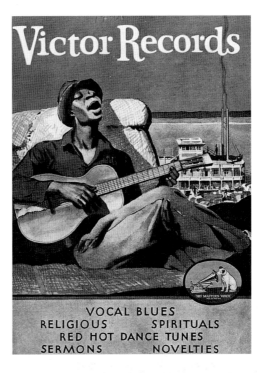

47 The Victor label, famous for its recordings of the Original Dixieland Jazz Band and Jelly Roll Morton, issued this catalogue of 'race records' in 1929 – the year in which the label was taken over by Radio Corporation of America (RCA).

Victor Records

VOCAL BLUES
RELIGIOUS   SPIRITUALS
RED HOT DANCE TUNES
SERMONS   NOVELTIES

By 1919 Marable's band had been joined by the young cornettist Louis Armstrong (1901–71), who was destined to become the most influential of all early jazz performers. Armstrong's lowly background in New Orleans was typical of many first-generation jazz musicians. His father was a labourer, who soon abandoned his family, while his mother was a prostitute. Born in a slum, young Louis gained his formative musical experiences in the bordellos of Storyville and by singing in street groups with friends. In 1913 he was removed to the Home for Colored Waifs when he fired a pistol into the air in high spirits on New Year's Day. However, his arrest at the age of twelve had a positive outcome, for it was at this institution that he was given the opportunity to learn the cornet. He already admired the playing of Buddy Bolden and Bunk Johnson, and now set out to emulate his idols by taking part in the brass band at the institution. The repertoire must have been typical of New Orleans band music in the second decade of the century: marches and ragtime, mixed with blues elements.

On his release, Armstrong resolved to pursue a career as a musician and owed his initial success to the timely patronage of King Oliver, who was then playing in an ensemble led by trombonist Kid Ory. In 1918, Oliver decided to follow the trend of relocating to Chicago, giving Armstrong the chance to fill the vacancy in Ory's band. Not long after, Armstrong also joined Marable's riverboat 'conservatoire'.

48 Mentor and protégé: Louis Armstrong and King Oliver around 1922.

49 An early publicity photograph of Armstrong, taken in Chicago in 1927.

However, Oliver had not forgotten his protégé, and Armstrong was invited in 1922 to join his mentor's Creole Jazz Band at the Lincoln Gardens in Chicago.

Armstrong was faced with a challenging task when he joined Oliver's band. In the New Orleans ensemble style it was difficult enough for the standard three-instrument front line to create convincing polyphony; the addition of a fourth melodic strand, which Armstrong was now asked to provide, caused further problems because his instrument was identical to Oliver's. This experience undoubtedly sharpened Armstrong's aural perception. As Gunther Schuller has demonstrated in an analysis in *Early Jazz* (1968), the countermelody Armstrong provided to Oliver's lead in their 1923 recording of *Mabel's Dream* on the Okeh label (one of the most important of the early independent record companies) is a striking example of Armstrong's innate ability to adapt improvised melodic shapes to the prevailing harmonic sequence. As Armstrong was in danger of upstaging his mentor with his virtuosity and musicality, it is not surprising, perhaps, that he did not stay with the Creole Jazz Band for long.

Armstrong's playing was characterized by a wide variety of original melodic and timbral devices that make his style instantly recognizable. Comparable formulae (subsequently known as 'licks' or 'signatures') would be used by countless later musicians as personal identifiers, forming in some cases a convenient stock of melodic clichés on which to fall back in moments of reduced inspiration. Armstrong's idiosyncratic mannerisms, adumbrated in his recordings with Oliver and developed in the later 1920s, include descending arpeggio patterns in triplets (a rhythmic device that became increasingly popular in jazz at the time), so-called 'rips' in which a high note is approached by an aggressive glissando, and a rich 'terminal vibrato' colouring sustained notes after the initial attack. His playing in these early years is distinguished by a powerful sense of swing, a characteristic that made him one of the 'hottest' performers of the time. (The term 'hot' in jazz originally referred to the rhythmic momentum of swung rhythm, at first the exclusive province of black performers.)

When Oliver's founding members began to disperse in 1924, Armstrong soon followed suit and quit – probably in response to pressure from his ambitious second wife, the band's pianist Lilian Hardin (1898–1971), who had studied music at Fisk University and went on to form her own band, The Dreamland Syncopators, in Chicago. Meanwhile, in 1924, Louis Armstrong set off for New York

50 Armstrong's Hot Five in 1925 (left to right): Louis Armstrong, Johnny St Cyr, Johnny Dodds, Kid Ory and Lil Armstrong.

to join the dance band led by pianist Fletcher Henderson. This influential group, which a few years later provided the direct model for the swing bands of the 1930s, gave Armstrong the opportunity to appear as featured soloist and to develop the improvisational skills that had such a profound influence on later jazz musicians. Many admired the apparent ease with which Armstrong began to construct his own balanced and sophisticated melodies when improvising on a given set of chords. A good example of his early solo style can be heard on Henderson's recording of *Sugarfoot Stomp* (May 1925), a reworking of King Oliver's *Dippermouth Blues*. Oliver's original had been named after Armstrong himself, whose capacious mouth earned him the affectionate nickname 'Satchmo', short for 'Satchelmouth'.

Armstrong learnt to read music fluently for the first time during his work with Henderson's band, and he in turn inspired them to play with a greater sense of swing. During his spell in New York, Armstrong broadened his horizons by recording five sides with blues singer Bessie Smith, including their masterful interpretation of W. C. Handy's *St Louis Blues*, and also cut sides with pianist Clarence Williams (1898–1965) and Sidney Bechet. The interpretation by Armstrong and Bechet of Williams's *Cake-Walkin' Babies from Home* (January 1925) perfectly matched the two instrumental virtuosos.

Returning to Chicago in the autumn of 1925, Armstrong formed with his wife the dynamic Hot Five and Hot Seven ensembles. The Hot Five comprised cornet or trumpet (Louis Armstrong), clarinet (Johnny Dodds) and trombone (Kid Ory) as its formidable front line,

51 An 'acoustic' recording session in the Okeh studios, Chicago, in 1925.

with a rhythm section of piano (Lil Armstrong) and banjo (Johnny St Cyr). The Hot Seven featured the same quintet with the addition of tuba (Pete Briggs) and drums (Baby Dodds). These groups arguably represent the peak of Armstrong's career and with them he achieved a standard of virtuosity he never surpassed. Without doubt, their epic series of recordings for the Okeh label from 1925 to 1928 are the high point of the New Orleans style. As a result of technological advances in the recording studio, they were also some of the first to be made with the electrical process, in which an amplified signal from a microphone replaced the primitive 'acoustic' horn.

At this time Armstrong started to abandon the 'paraphrase' approach, in which a performer constructed a solo simply by embellishing the basic melody, while leaving the theme recognizable for the most part. Instead, he began to create fresh melodies above the repeating harmonies of the piece (called 'the changes' by jazz musicians), and managed to shape his melodic patterns with a coherence and sense of symmetrical balance worthy of a classical composer. Armstrong's technique of matching each of his two- or four-bar melodic phrases to the immediately preceding phrase – known as the 'correlated chorus',

68

a term coined by the young trumpeter Bix Beiderbecke – imparted an organic sense of growth to the whole melody. Remarkably, and in sharp contrast to classical music, this melodic sophistication appears to have been achieved spontaneously. In promoting the extended improvised solo as the core of a performance, Armstrong laid the foundations for almost all subsequent jazz.

Armstrong's improvisational skills were complemented by an impressive virtuosity on his instrument, which he changed in 1926 from cornet to trumpet in pursuit of a more brilliant sonority. His agility in negotiating rapid passagework had already been demonstrated in his recordings with King Oliver, and at times he broke with convention by playing in double time (twice as fast as everyone else) to increase tension. Further excitement was generated by Armstrong's breaks, which sometimes departed radically from the harmonies at that point in the piece. His range expanded and he hit top Cs with breathtaking ease. (These thrilling upper pitches were considerably higher than King Oliver's top notes; in fact, they were well above the highest clarinet notes produced by Dodds in the Oliver

52 From the 1930s, Armstrong's talents as a singer and popular entertainer brought him considerable commercial success.

sessions.) His daring led him to extend cross-rhythms for considerably longer durations than any previous musician, sometimes cutting across the regular underlying metre for an entire section before converging again with the main beats. All these innovations were widely imitated by later trumpeters, including Dizzy Gillespie and even Miles Davis; Armstrong's improvisational methods were also adapted for use on other instruments.

Among the most influential of the Hot Five recordings were *Cornet Chop Suey* (1926) and *West End Blues* (1928). In the former, an entire section consists of a succession of increasingly irregular solo breaks above a 'stop-time' texture. (In this technique from New Orleans jazz, the rhythm section abruptly falls silent to throw the soloist into sharp relief and fulfils a punctuating rather than accompanying function. It was put to good use in the Hot Five's 1927 recording of *Potato Head Blues*.) *West End Blues* begins with a stunning cadenza for unaccompanied trumpet, radical for its time and much imitated by later adherents of the Armstrong style. The music then builds in intensity from a lyrical beginning reminiscent of the New Orleans marching bands, through a gradual rise in pitch to the climactic final section, in which Armstrong sustains a riveting high note for no fewer than four slow bars.

Armstrong's talents were not restricted to trumpet playing: he also began to make a name for himself as an accomplished singer, especially in the 'scat' style. This technique, made famous by Armstrong in the Hot Five recordings of *Heebie Jeebies* (1926) and *Hotter Than That* (1927), involved singing nonsense syllables to an improvised melody. He allegedly introduced the technique on the spur of the moment when he dropped his music during a rehearsal and was unable to remember the words, but it seems more likely that scat singing had originated earlier in New Orleans. Indeed, Jelly Roll Morton claimed the credit for its invention. The significance of Armstrong's scatting lies in his skilful vocal adaptation of the resourceful style of his instrumental improvisations. In 1925 he had matched sung blues inflections and melodic patterns on the cornet when accompanying Bessie Smith; the process was now reversed as his singing took on instrumental characteristics. The close identification of vocal and instrumental styles in jazz from this point onwards was assured. Armstrong's impure but warm and characterful singing voice – often described as 'gravelly' – was an early example of the 'dirty' tone favoured in jazz, and influenced the singing of Fats Waller and Billie Holiday.

53 Earl Hines sits opposite singer Sarah Vaughan (second piano) in New York's Apollo Theater in 1943. His band includes bop stars Dizzy Gillespie (far left) and Charlie Parker (far right).

Lil Armstrong was replaced in some later Hot Five recordings by Earl 'Fatha' Hines (1903–83), who had been working with Armstrong and violinist Carroll Dickerson at Chicago's Sunset Café since 1926. In 1928, Hines contributed a piano solo to *West End Blues*, and at the end of the same year cut an extraordinary duet with Armstrong based on King Oliver's composition *Weather Bird*. The stylistic distance travelled by jazz in the five years since Oliver's Creole Jazz Band recorded the piece is stupendous. Armstrong and Hines trade improvised melodic and rhythmic ideas with consummate ease, sometimes diverging into independent rhythmic patterns of considerable complexity, then converging at structurally important moments: what was originally a standard tripartite post-ragtime piece has been transformed into a masterpiece founded on an intuitive rapport between two of the finest musicians of their age.

54 Hines in later years: a keyboard player of dazzling inventiveness and flexibility.

Hines's piano playing moved away from the restrictions of the stride school, adapting Armstrong's melodic idiom and double-time passages to create the 'trumpet style' of piano playing (in which the melody is often stated in octaves by the right hand). He also emulated Armstrong's sophisticated use of syncopation and swing, sometimes making his hands pursue quite independent rhythmic patterns. Hines remained in Chicago when Armstrong left for New York in 1929, and formed a band at the Grand Terrace Ballroom, a favourite haunt of the Mafia. His band gained considerable popularity through radio broadcasts in the 1930s and he successfully adapted his music to the demands of the swing-band style then fashionable. He continued to make innovations in keyboard technique: his later recordings included an ingenious mixture of glissandos, arpeggios, trills and cross-rhythms.

The final flowering of the Hot Five in 1928 coincided with a crucial turning point in the history of jazz. The centre of gravity for musicians shifted from Chicago to New York, which was establishing its reputation as the popular-music capital of the world with the new swing style. During the years of Prohibition (1920–33), Chicago became a centre for the illicit alcohol trade sponsored by the city's infamous gangster community. Musicians began to drift eastwards after the official clampdown on illegal drinking that closed many Chicago nightspots in 1928. King Oliver had been in New York since 1927, and Jelly Roll Morton arrived the following year: both masters of the New Orleans style rapidly fell victim to changing fashions. Armstrong's talents proved to be more adaptable to public tastes when he moved to New York in 1929: he became a celebrity by singing 'Ain't Misbehavin'' in Fats Waller's Broadway show *Hot Chocolates*. This marked the start of his career as a highly paid popular entertainer, and the beginning of his much-lamented 'sellout' to commercial interests.

55 Armstrong (far left) at a 1940s *Esquire* concert, featuring drummer 'Big' Sid Catlett (far right).

Armstrong was by no means the only prominent jazz musician to secure for himself a lucrative career in the entertainment industry. Nat 'King' Cole instigated the innovative genre of the piano trio and then defected to the world of popular song and television shows, and even Miles Davis – who felt Armstrong's self-conscious cultivation of the stereotyped image of a grinning Negro entertainer was little short of treason against the black race, and an embarrassing reminder of demeaning minstrelsy – laid himself open to similar charges of commercialism when promoting jazz-rock fusion in the 1970s. However much Armstrong is criticized for his 'sellout', it did at least secure his career throughout the harsh years of the Depression when record sales dwindled dramatically.

As a result of his transatlantic tours of 1933 and 1934, Armstrong's fame spread to Europe. Back in New York in 1935, he hired the hard-hitting agent Joe Glaser, who placed him in Luis Russell's band alongside several former New Orleans colleagues. Film appearances and a popular radio show made him a household name, but did little to develop his once highly original musical style. His repertoire increasingly embraced sentimental popular songs, and for a time he modified his voice to sound like the suave 'crooners' who were then in vogue; his trumpet playing fell back on familiar and sometimes predictable licks and melodic formulae. In 1944 he appeared at the old Metropolitan Opera House in New York in a concert held by *Esquire* magazine, and recorded numerous sides on the 'V'-discs manufactured for American troops serving overseas.

When the big-band craze evaporated after World War II, Armstrong returned to the traditional style of small-ensemble jazz then enjoying a revival, in a performance at Town Hall, New York, in 1947. The six-piece group formed for this occasion was subsequently billed by Glaser as the 'All Stars'. In 1948 Hines joined the group, but his relationship with Armstrong soon grew strained and he quit after three years. Until a heart attack in 1959 forced him to slow down, Armstrong performed and recorded with the All Stars to widespread acclaim. He had become a national institution, a status formally acknowledged when 'Ambassador Satch' was sent by the US State Department on a series of high-profile worldwide tours.

55

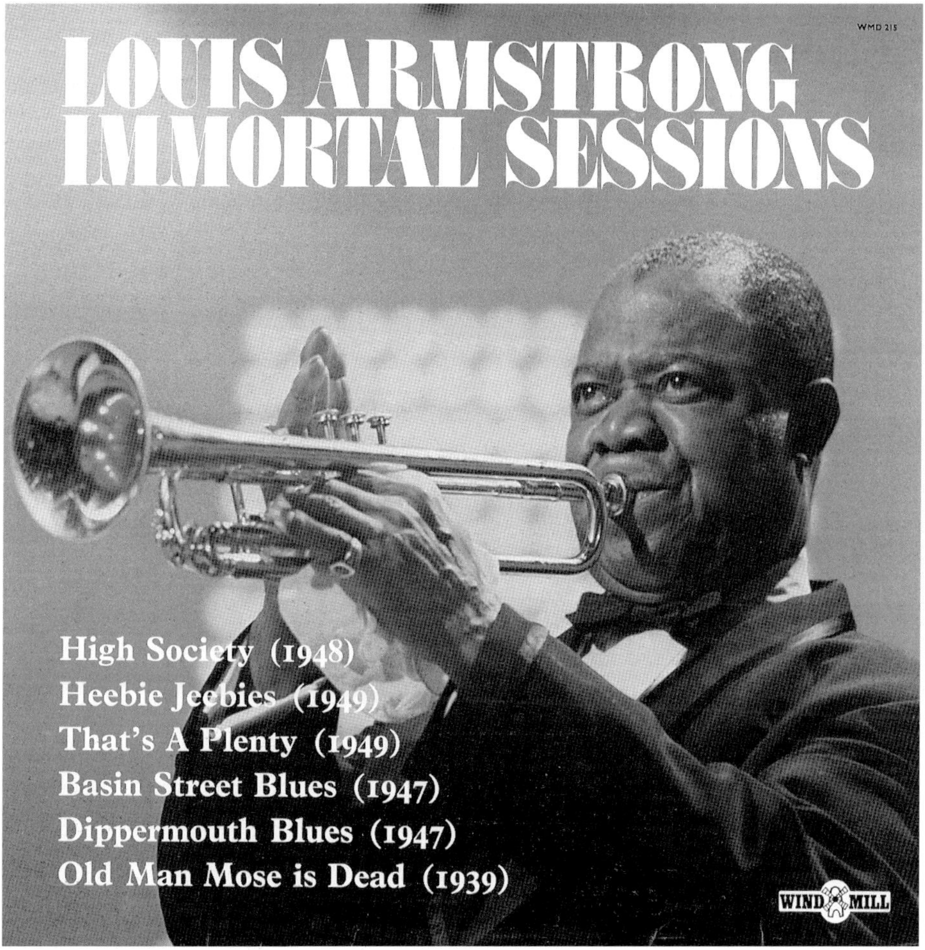

LOUIS ARMSTRONG IMMORTAL SESSIONS

WMD 215

High Society (1948)
Heebie Jeebies (1949)
That's A Plenty (1949)
Basin Street Blues (1947)
Dippermouth Blues (1947)
Old Man Mose is Dead (1939)

WIND MILL

56 An LP re-release of Armstrong hits from the 1940s.

CHAPTER FIVE

The Rise and Fall of the Big Band

In the 1930s popular music and classical music came closer together than they have been in any period of history, and, in some cases, they even stylistically merged. The global exposure that jazz assured for itself in the aptly named 'Swing Era' (*c.* 1928–45) made it the popular music of the war years, and it is arguable that, neither before nor since, has pop music had such universal appeal or such high artistic quality. Since the 1950s, pop, jazz and classical genres have branched out in different directions, but for a few golden years between the wars they seemed to find common ground.

When King Oliver, Jelly Roll Morton and Louis Armstrong arrived in New York at the end of the 1920s, they entered a very different musical environment from early New Orleans. Jazz performers and composers on the East Coast were, on the whole, better educated and had higher artistic ambitions: their aspirations were typified by the flourishing school of Harlem stride pianists, who dressed elegantly and borrowed freely from the techniques of classical music – and who apparently thought very little of Morton's piano playing. Although some jazz in the up-tempo Chicago version of the New Orleans style could still be heard in New York, its popularity was dwindling. Both Oliver and Morton, masters of the old style, sank into obscurity after 1929 because their musical language had little in common with the big-band idiom that supplanted it. The music of the Swing Era sprang from a different source: the dance band.

57 Count Basie (bottom, third from right) and his band board a Scandinavian Airlines flight during their first European tour in March 1954.

By the mid-1920s, New York dance bands had earned themselves fame and a healthy income by providing exactly what the wider public craved: easy, polished dance music with a sense of swing and an elegant sophistication in instrumental colour, but few of the rougher and more subversive characteristics of early jazz such as extensive improvisation, earthy blues numbers or 'dirty' sonorities. The dance bands continued a lively popular-music tradition that went back to successful ragtime orchestras such as that led by James Reese Europe (1881–1919). His famous Society Orchestra, which in 1913 became the first black group to make recordings, had included stringed instruments – principally violins and mandolins, but sometimes cellos. The sonorities produced by these instruments had a closer association with classical music than with New Orleans ensemble jazz, and violins in particular were retained as a fundamental section of many later dance bands.

The dance orchestras began to absorb some of the innovations of early jazz, including blue notes, twelve-bar blues structures, swung rhythm and short improvised passages for solo instruments. However, in more fundamental stylistic terms the dance bands remained very different from the New Orleans ensembles. Whereas the New Orleans style had been based on the combination of several independent melodic lines derived from the same theme, the dance bands tended to present a single melodic line in block-chord harmonization. The most distinctive sound of big-band jazz – a sinuous melody harmonized in block chords by a group of saxophones or brass – was a direct development from the procedure popularized by the dance bands and essentially had little to do with the New Orleans style. The New Orleans groups had elaborated simple harmonic schemes borrowed from ragtime and the blues, mostly comprising a few basic chords, but dance bands made extensive use of sophisticated harmonies imported from classical music. As the harmonic idiom of jazz became more complex, the viability of the New Orleans approach diminished: the Dixieland and swing-band styles were essentially incompatible.

White dance bands achieved greater commercial success, although several black groups were undoubtedly their superior in artistic terms. One of the finest white orchestras was that led by pianist Jean Goldkette (1899–1962). Based in Detroit but recording mostly in New York, Goldkette's orchestra is best remembered for its collaboration with the prodigious cornettist Bix Beiderbecke (1903–31), the first white performer to be widely regarded by black musicians as their

58 Bix Beiderbecke (fourth from right), pictured with The Wolverines in 1924.

artistic equal. Beiderbecke's premature death from alcoholism made him one of the most poignant casualties of the Prohibition years. Initially inspired by the work of Nick LaRocca with the Original Dixieland Jazz Band, Beiderbecke had formed a group modelled on the New Orleans Rhythm Kings in Chicago in 1924. Two years later he was hired by Goldkette to provide 'hot' solo passages as a contrast to largely pre-composed band accompaniments. Pleasing but intellectually undemanding arrangements such as the version of *Blue River* recorded by Goldkette in 1927 show that their style became the basis for the 1930s Hollywood musical. In contrast to Armstrong, Beiderbecke cultivated a mellow cornet tone which he varied for sonorous effect only to a small degree, relying for expressive power on an innate lyricism expressed in delicately balanced phrases. He was also a talented pianist and composer: his piano piece *In a Mist* (1927), with its advanced harmonies reminiscent of French impressionism, reveals his debt to Debussy and classical music.

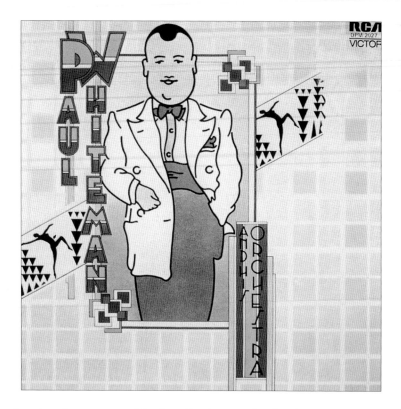

Another important white bandleader was Paul Whiteman (1890–1967), whose orchestra Beiderbecke joined in 1927 after Goldkette suffered financial difficulties. Whiteman had made a very successful recording in 1920 of a banal, old-fashioned and sentimental piece called *Whispering*, which sold more than a million copies, and his orchestra epitomized the pre-composed and highly popular jazzy dance music of its age. His arrangements, which could be pretentious, sometimes made incongruous allusions to classical music, including Rachmaninov's Prelude in C sharp minor in *Hot Lips* (1922) and Grieg's 'Hall of the Mountain King' at the start of a 1926 recording of *St Louis Blues*. Nevertheless, Whiteman's scores were distinguished by a thorough grasp of harmony and often inventive orchestration. Some early sides imitate the New Orleans polyphonic style, but his music never exhibited the improvisational freedom characteristic of authentic jazz. As a result, many black musicians resented his popular nickname 'The King of Jazz', which was taken from a 1930 Hollywood film celebrating his achievements.

59 An RCA Victor LP
release of Paul Whiteman's
popular dance music.

60 George Gershwin
(left) and Whiteman,
with whom he
collaborated on the
influential *Rhapsody
in Blue* in 1924.

In 1924 Whiteman gained notoriety when he promoted a bold 'Experiment in Modern Music': a concert work for piano and band composed by George Gershwin (1898–1937), which set out to combine elements of jazz and classical music. The resulting *Rhapsody in Blue*, first performed by the composer with Whiteman's band at the Aeolian Hall, New York, in February 1924, had a far-reaching influence scarcely commensurate with its (by Gershwin's standards) mediocre quality. 'Symphonic jazz' became widely imitated, and Gershwin himself went on to produce more satisfying essays in the new style, including a Piano Concerto (1925), the symphonic poem *An American in Paris* (1928) and his 'American folk opera' *Porgy and Bess* (1935), which donated several songs to the growing repertory of jazz standards – among them the enduringly popular 'Summertime'.

Symphonic jazz also became a vehicle for the growing nationalist trend in American classical music. On his return to New York in 1924 from studies in Paris, Aaron Copland (1900–90) composed jazz-inspired works, such as *Music for the Theater* (1925) and his Piano

81

61 Fletcher Henderson's orchestra in New York in the autumn of 1924. Its members include Coleman Hawkins and Louis Armstrong (second and third from left); Henderson is behind the bass drum and Don Redman on the far right.

Concerto (1927), featuring saxophones and percussionists imitating a drum kit. Although Copland later abandoned the idiom in favour of a nationalism more rooted in North American folk music, these early scores were a model for the young Leonard Bernstein (1918–90), who brought symphonic jazz to its peak.

By far the most important precursor of big-band jazz was the ensemble led by black pianist Fletcher Henderson (1897–1952). Although less successful commercially than either Goldkette or Whiteman, Henderson – who also had an intimate knowledge of classical music – managed to integrate 'hot' jazz elements into his dance arrangements. His band came to public attention in 1924 when it began playing at the Club Alabam on Broadway and then at the Roseland Ballroom, the foremost dancing venue in New York (where on one occasion the Goldkette and Henderson orchestras indulged in a cutting contest). Henderson hired Louis Armstrong as featured soloist for a short spell from 1924 to 1925. Armstrong's virtuosic improvisations and infectious swung rhythm transformed the band's playing and he was a clear influence on Henderson's tenor saxophonist Coleman Hawkins (1904–69), who adopted the trumpeter's manner of melodic construction. Hawkins became one of the greatest saxophonists of the Swing Era, recording in 1939 an intensely lyrical interpretation of *Body and Soul* that set a new standard of improvisation for his formerly neglected instrument.

In addition to the strengths of his featured soloists, Henderson assembled an impressive repertoire of arrangements prepared both by himself and by the talented Don Redman (1900–64). Redman laid the foundations for the big-band style, which integrates genuinely improvised solo sections with pre-composed passages for the full band; the latter are skilfully constructed in a pseudo-improvised style to sound spontaneous, but the music is predetermined and notated in the performing parts (known as 'charts'). In the mid-1920s the Henderson orchestra comprised three trumpets, one trombone (a

62 Coleman Hawkins in the 1940s, at the time he was playing with the young Miles Davis (right) in 52nd Street clubs.

second was added in 1927), three saxophones (doubling as clarinets) and a variable four-piece rhythm section (piano, banjo or guitar, doublebass or tuba, and drums); the absence of strings immediately gave the ensemble a jazzier sound than that produced by the Whiteman and Goldkette bands. Redman based his arrangements on block-chord technique, alternating passages scored for reeds with similar passages for brass to create an exciting antiphonal music reflecting the 'call-and-response' patterns so fundamental to jazz. The harmonies were more complex than those in the New Orleans style, showing the continuing influence of classical music.

Another important device was the 'riff', essentially a simple but catchy melodic motif repeated over and over again (known in classical music as an *ostinato*, from the Italian word for 'obstinate'). Riffs had two functions in the big-band style: either they were played softly in the background to support a solo improvisation, or they became the main melody itself. The energetic trading of riffs between reeds and brass in rapid call-and-response patterns became one of the most appealing features of big-band jazz.

Taking the Henderson orchestra as their model, the big bands of the Swing Era expanded their instrumental sections, so that by the mid-1930s a typical line-up comprised three or four trumpets, three trombones, four (later five) saxophones and the standard four-piece rhythm section. These bands continued to make use of the block chords and riff patterns of the Redman-Henderson arrangements, although they started to develop two other techniques that have survived to the present day. The aptly named 'walking bass' was a more active bass line, which left the march-style basses of early jazz far behind and filled out the intervals between the harmony notes to create an independent melodic line, mostly striding along in even note-values. When it is skilfully executed, the walking bass adds considerably to both the rhythmic momentum and harmonic direction of a piece. Less important but even more recognizable were the simple, repetitive rhythmic patterns performed with a drumstick on the 'hi-hat', a pair of parallel cymbals held horizontally on a stand and closed by a foot pedal on alternate beats. Both developments encouraged performers to play with a greater sense of the swung rhythm that gives jazz its characteristic energy.

63 Don Redman, photographed here in the 1930s, pioneered the techniques of big-band arrangement in his work with Fletcher Henderson.

64 The Benny Goodman Quartet in 1937 (left to right): Lionel Hampton, Teddy Wilson, Goodman and Gene Krupa.

Henderson's band entered a dark period in 1934 when Hawkins left to work with bandleader Jack Hylton at the BBC in London. As Goldkette had before him, Henderson faced financial difficulties and was forced to sell some of his arrangements to make ends meet. In 1934 a young Jewish clarinettist, Benny Goodman (1909–86), bought some of Henderson's orchestrations for his new band with funding made available by a National Broadcasting Company (NBC) radio show, for which the band had successfully auditioned. Goodman began making a name for himself in July 1935 when he recorded trio sides with drummer Gene Krupa (1909–73) and pianist Teddy Wilson (1912–86). These recordings are important not only as early examples of the chamber-music jazz that later replaced the big bands after World War II, but also for Goodman's use of mixed-race personnel: Krupa was white and Wilson black. In 1936 Goodman added the black vibraphone player Lionel Hampton (b. 1908) to the group to create a racially balanced quartet that recorded a famous and delicate rendering of *Moonglow*.

86

65 Philips's LP reissue of Goodman's legendary concert at New York's Carnegie Hall on 16 January 1938.

In the summer of 1935, Goodman's twelve-strong band (identical in instrumentation to Henderson's orchestra of 1927) embarked on its first national tour. On 21 August their music was broadcast live in front of an ecstatic crowd at the Palomar Ballroom in Los Angeles and became an overnight sensation. Goodman and his band were the hottest property in the ensuing craze for the 'new' (actually several years old) swing music. Such were the commercial advantages enjoyed by white musicians at the time: Henderson, with his performances of precisely the same arrangements, had failed to gain national prominence. Recognizing Henderson's contribution to his phenomenal success, however, Goodman secured his services as the band's full-time arranger in 1939.

Goodman's 1935 version of Jelly Roll Morton's *King Porter Stomp*, based on an arrangement by Henderson, is one of the best-known recordings of the era. Morton's piece had started life around 1906 as a piano rag that culminated in a 'hot' section with dissonant blue notes, prototype riffs and an implied call-and-response pattern. Henderson's arrangement exploited these devices, which had become fundamental to the swing style, but wisely re-composed the opening section (which would have sounded dated in the late 1920s). In a subsequent version, entitled *New King Porter Stomp* (1932), the first section was compressed almost beyond recognition; it was this arrangement that Goodman popularized.

65 Within three years of his initial success in Los Angeles, Goodman commanded sufficient respect to mount a jazz concert at Carnegie Hall in New York. This epoch-making event, which took place on 16 January 1938, was the first time jazz had been performed at a classical venue and its significance in raising the music to a new level of intellectual respectability cannot be overemphasized. Goodman constructed a well-balanced programme designed to reflect the development of jazz over the previous twenty years: from this point onwards, jazz was taken seriously by both critics and historians. The second part of the concert began with a parody of the Original Dixieland Jazz Band, in which Gene Krupa supplied appropriately crude drumming, and included an imitation of Armstrong's introductory cadenza style by trumpeter Harry James (1916–83). The climax was a fourteen-minute 'jam session' (group improvisation: the term had to be explained to the Carnegie audience in their programme notes) based on Fats Waller's *Honeysuckle Rose*. It was performed by an ensemble that included, in addition to Goodman and James, some of the biggest names in jazz at the time: Duke Ellington's saxophonists Johnny Hodges and Harry Carney, pianist Count Basie and his saxophonist Lester Young. Nearly a quarter of an hour of uninterrupted jazz improvisation from musicians of this calibre was an experience quite new to an audience who probably thought that jazz was restricted to the three-minute format imposed by limitations in 78 r.p.m. recording technology.

In December 1938, record producer John Hammond (1910–87) mounted another concert at Carnegie Hall under the title 'From Spirituals to Swing', featuring neglected boogie-woogie pianists with such success that the famous Blue Note record label was founded soon after to record their performances for posterity. Goodman returned to the Carnegie stage for a second concert in October 1939. Links between the newly respectable jazz and classical music were furthered by Goodman's blossoming career as both jazz and classical clarinettist. He recorded Mozart's Clarinet Quintet in 1938, and went on to commission works from Béla Bartók, Benjamin Britten, Aaron Copland and Paul Hindemith.

Several successful bandleaders began their careers as sidemen to Goodman, including the flamboyant drummer Gene Krupa, who left the band in 1938 after the relationship between the two egocentric personalities broke down. In the mid-1950s Krupa set up a conservatory of percussion in New York with Cozy Cole (1906–81), who had played for the big band fronted by popular singer Cab Calloway (1907–94) in the war years. Goodman's lead trumpeter Harry James, whose virtuosity was inspired by Armstrong, also quit in 1938 after two years with the band and became a popular idol; in the late 1950s he brought big-band jazz back into the limelight with a success comparable only to that of Count Basie. The vibraphone player Lionel Hampton, Goodman's former quartet colleague, founded his own band in 1940 and produced a smash hit with *Flying Home* two years later. Hampton's band, which undertook numerous worldwide tours from the 1950s onwards, is the longest surviving big band in the history of jazz.

66 Originally a drummer, Lionel Hampton recorded a vibraphone solo in 1930 and soon established himself as the instrument's first virtuoso.

67 Lester Young, pictured here shortly before his death, developed a light and lyrical style of saxophone playing that influenced the next generation of performers.

68 Count Basie in 1956, when his second big band was the leading light in post-war swing.

During the 1930s the popularity of commercial white bands from New York masked the fact that the best music in the swing-band idiom was already being produced by black ensembles – by now a depressingly familiar state of affairs. Apart from the remarkable achievements of Duke Ellington, who had moved from his native Washington, DC, to New York in 1923, the most important black bands emerged from Kansas City, Missouri, in the early 1920s. Pianist Bennie Moten (1894–1935) had the foresight to hire fellow stride exponent William 'Count' Basie (1904–84) in 1929 as his future successor to lead a fine band, which produced music similar to Henderson's in New York but reflecting a greater blues influence. Their 'southwest' style tended to favour less complex arrangements than those popular on the East Coast, a more prominent use of saxophones and a higher degree of improvisation (and, hence, spontaneity): in short, the style was jazzier, and swung with considerable rhythmic drive. Basie temporarily assumed control of the band on Moten's death, then formed his own group with some of the most capable members of the original ensemble, including saxophonists Lester Young (1909–59) and Herschel Evans (1909–39). Basie's band, originally comprising nine men, strengthened the walking bass and hi-hat rhythm of swing, and promoted a regular four-beat pulse of considerable power: its work was destined to remain rooted in the twelve-bar blues for many decades.

90

Basie might well have languished in Kansas City if he had not been discovered by Hammond in 1936 and brought to New York in an attempt to capitalize on the vogue for swing. The Basie band established itself at Henderson's former haunt, the Roseland Ballroom, in 1937. In the same year, the group had a hit with *One o'clock Jump*, a twelve-bar blues piece that ends with a good example of an energetic riff. It was at this time that the incomparable singer Billie Holiday joined the band, though she was prevented from recording with it for contractual reasons. The association nurtured her enduring spiritual and musical affinity with Lester Young. Apart from a brief interruption from 1950 to 1952, owing to financial difficulties, Basie's orchestra continued to go from strength to strength and in the late 1950s it was still producing the best jazz of any conventional big band. Its flugelhorn player Thad Jones (1923–86), a skilful arranger who formed a large virtuoso ensemble with drummer Mel Lewis in 1965, secured a creative future for big-band music – based firmly on the Basie style – into the 1960s and beyond.

Other black bandleaders of note were the hunchback drummer Chick Webb (1909–38), whose orchestra played at the Savoy Ballroom in New York and featured the teenage Ella Fitzgerald; Jimmie Lunceford (1902–47), who made his name at the famous Cotton Club, New York, in 1934 and remained influential until 1942, when a pay dispute caused his band's near collapse; suave and nimble-fingered pianist Teddy Wilson, who left Goodman's trio and quartet in 1939 to form a band featuring Billie Holiday and Lester Young; and Armstrong's former pianist Earl Hines, who put the Grand Terrace, Chicago, on the map as a centre for exuberant swing-band jazz.

Popular white leaders included clarinettists Woody Herman (1913–87) and Artie Shaw (b. 1910). Herman named his bands 'Herds' and they were sufficiently virtuosic to inspire Stravinsky to compose his *Ebony Concerto* for them in 1945. This work, described by its composer as a 'jazz concerto grosso', directly influenced the symphonic-jazz style of Bernstein, who four years later composed his *Prelude, Fugue and Riffs* for Herman (although its first performance was not given until 1955 by Goodman in a television broadcast). Shaw recorded his hit *Begin the Beguine* in 1938 before retiring less than a year later; he joined the US Navy in January 1942, one month after the Japanese attack on Pearl Harbor sent America to war, and toured the Pacific with a new group. The most famous wartime band was that led by trombonist Glenn Miller (1904–44), who enlisted as a captain in the US Army Air Force, and rose to the rank of major. Miller's band travelled to Europe to entertain American troops, and it was on 15 December 1944, while flying from London to Paris in poor weather, that he and his aircraft disappeared.

69 Igor Stravinsky directs Woody Herman and his Herd in a rehearsal of the *Ebony Concerto* in 1946.

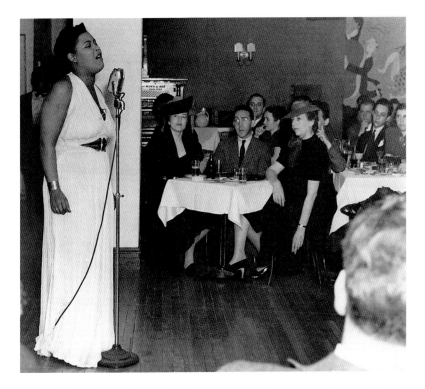

70 Billie Holiday starts her month-long engagement at Café Society in Greenwich Village, New York, in April 1939. The controversial club's motto was 'The Wrong Place for the Right People'.

If it seems regrettable to categorize bands according to the skin colour of their personnel, an incident in 1939 demonstrated that racial tensions in jazz were still only just beneath the surface. At Café Society, New York, Billie Holiday drew large mixed-race audiences in 1939 with her deeply affecting rendering of *Strange Fruit*, a song about lynching in the Deep South with a disturbing text by Lewis Allan that graphically described the hanging and burning of black victims. When issued on disc, this extraordinary song was banned by many radio stations in America and by the BBC in London.

The rapid decline in the popularity of big-band jazz after 1945 was caused by several factors. The drastic series of recording bans imposed by James Caesar Petrillo's American Federation of Musicians (AFM) in an attempt to secure royalties on radio broadcasts badly affected its

71 A Royal Air Force band entertains 'in the field' during World War II.

members' livelihoods from 1942 to 1944, and again in 1948. More importantly, however, the big-band style had grown sterile in the hands of many of its less inspired but often commercially successful practitioners. One example was Glenn Miller, whose music was rarely enlivened by a genuine sense of swing and took the block-chord voicing typical of the era to a sometimes insupportable extreme, as in the sentimental reed doublings of his *Moonlight Serenade* (1939). The latter, together with the equally famous *In the Mood* (also recorded in 1939), secured Miller an enviably constant position at the top of the record charts. His very success represented the parting of the ways between jazz and the growing popular-music industry, which continued to be characterized by an artistic superficiality caused largely by white commercial over-exploitation of the big-band idiom.

Big bands managed to survive changing fashions – if at times precariously. They employed featured soloists who were versed in the new 'be-bop' style that began to emerge in the early 1940s, an importation which the essentially sectionalized structure of swing music easily permitted. So-called 'progressive jazz' was developed by Stan Kenton (1911–79), whose Innovations in Modern Music Orchestra explored an intriguing but sometimes pretentious and stilted mixture of big-band jazz and pseudo-classical music. Affection for genuine big-band jazz doggedly persisted and when Benny Goodman (fronting a much younger band) played at Carnegie Hall on 17 January 1978 to mark the fortieth anniversary of his historic first appearance there, the band's energetic rendering of Henderson's time-honoured arrangement of Morton's *King Porter Stomp* still brought the house down.

72 Stan Kenton, whose innovative big band nurtured an impressive roster of West Coast talent in the 1950s.

CHAPTER SIX

The Composer: Duke Ellington

The work of Jelly Roll Morton had shown as early as the mid-1920s that jazz was capable of sustaining intellectual interest: as with all music of quality, it could be appreciated on both an emotional and an analytical level, according to the listener's sensibilities and musical expertise. By the time of Goodman's Carnegie Hall concert in 1938, several critical studies of jazz had been published as a testament to the music's new-found respectability. These books appeared not in America but in Europe, where jazz was still in its infancy in the early 1930s. The most influential of the early monographs was Hugues Panassié's *Le Jazz hot*, which appeared in Paris in 1934. Two years later, Charles Delaunay, son of the painters Robert and Sonia Delaunay, published in the same city his *Hot Discography*, the first listing of jazz records to appear in print.

In 1934, the English composer Constant Lambert (1905–51) included in his provocative book *Music Ho!: A Study of Music in Decline* a section devoted to the work of Edward Kennedy 'Duke' Ellington (1899–1974). Rarely lavish with his praise, Lambert was nevertheless in no doubt about the artistic significance of Ellington's compositions and his comments deserve quotation at some length:

> An artist like Louis Armstrong, who is one of the most remarkable virtuosi of the present day, enthrals us at a first hearing, but after a few records one realizes that all his improvisations are based on the same restricted circle of ideas... The best records of Duke Ellington, on the other hand, can be listened to again and again because they are not just decorations of a familiar shape but a new arrangement of shapes. Ellington, in fact, is a real composer, the first jazz composer of distinction, and the first Negro composer of distinction. His works – apart from a few minor details – are not left to the caprice or ear of the instrumentalist; they are scored and written out, and though, in the course of time, variants may creep in...the first American records of his music may be taken definitively...and are the only jazz records worth studying for their form as well as their texture...

73 Count Basie and Duke Ellington at the time of their collaborative recordings in the early 1960s.

Although Lambert was inevitably influenced by his training as a classical composer, so that he placed a greater value on pre-composition than on improvisation, he succinctly expounds Ellington's stature as the first composer in jazz to have created musical structures worthy of direct comparison with classical music. Ellington was equally sceptical about the artistic value of improvisation, and his comments in an article published in 1958 appear to echo Lambert's sentiments:'It is my firm belief that there has never been anybody who has blown even two bars worth listening to who didn't have some idea of what he was going to play, before he started... There has to be some thought preceding each phrase, otherwise it is meaningless.' It was a theme to which he returned in his autobiography, published in 1973, although in those later years praise for his achievements had become so universal that he no doubt felt few qualms about discussing his own brand of jazz in terms more appropriate to classical techniques.

Ellington's formative years in Washington, DC, were typical: like most future pianist-bandleaders, such as Bennie Moten, Count Basie and Fletcher Henderson, he spent his adolescence absorbing the ragtime and stride styles, and developed a competent if not virtuosic keyboard technique. In 1919 he joined forces with the precocious drummer Sonny Greer (1895–1982), with whom he visited New York in 1922, though he initially failed to make his mark. In the following year, however, he returned to the city and benefited from the patronage of three giants of the stride-piano school: Willie 'The Lion' Smith, James P. Johnson and Fats Waller. By 1924, Ellington and Greer were playing in Harlem and on Broadway with Elmer Snowden's band, The Washingtonians, and were making their first recordings. Ellington replaced Snowden (1900–73) as leader in the same year, and began to ▶ assemble a remarkable group of instrumentalists who were an important factor in the band's later success.

Ellington's entrepreneurial and artistic skills resulted in what has become universally known as 'the Ellington effect' – a musical phenomenon that almost defies verbal description. On the one hand, Ellington assembled around him a collection of fine performers, each of whose playing was marked by clearly recognizable idiosyncrasies that allowed their solo passages to be distinctively characterized; several also composed and contributed their ideas to the band's growing repertoire. On the other hand, Ellington's consummate abilities as an orchestrator allowed him to blend these individual sonorities ('sound identities', as he himself termed them) in fluctuating ensemble colours of radical originality. The analogy between this compositional

74 Duke Ellington (far right) with The Washingtonians at the Kentucky Club, New York, in 1924. The cluster of instruments in front of drummer Sonny Greer (far left) is typical of posed publicity shots of the era.

process and the manner in which a painter blends pigments on a palette to produce subtle shades may be clichéd, but it is in this case perfectly accurate. As Lambert put it: 'The real interest of Ellington's records lies not so much in their colour, brilliant though it may be, as in the amazingly skilful proportions in which the colour is used.'

The first notable addition to Ellington's band was trumpeter Bubber Miley (1903–32), who joined in 1923 and whose blues-based manner of playing had a strong influence on the group during the six years he spent with it. Miley's major innovation in jazz trumpet playing was the so-called 'growl' technique, which became a hallmark of the Ellington style. It aimed to capture the rough, expressive sound of blues singing by employing a variety of devices simultaneously: two mutes (one metal, inserted in the bell of the instrument, and the other a rubber plunger held over it and moved around to vary the tone in

99

the manner of a 'wah-wah' mute) combined with throat noises, hummed pitches and the instrument's own basic note. This elaborate method of tone-production was adapted for the trombone by Joe 'Tricky Sam' Nanton (1904–46), who joined the band in 1926 and became famous for 'yah-yah' solos in which his playing sounded uncannily like a human voice.

In 1927, the Ellington orchestra, now comprising ten performers, began a highly successful residency at the Cotton Club in Harlem. This venue, which had opened in 1923, could seat a (strictly white) audience of approximately seven hundred, who were entertained by black dancers performing various exotic routines in elaborate costumes on lavish stage sets. Ellington's four-year stay at the Cotton Club furthered his career in two ways. First, a series of nightly radio broadcasts from the venue secured him an extensive popular following. Secondly, and more importantly, the wide variety of stage routines for which he was required to provide music compelled him to explore a wider range of compositional styles than other bands producing a steady stream of music designed exclusively for public dancing. Three categories of music that Ellington tackled at the Cotton Club with great resourcefulness were 'mood' pieces with a blues flavour, abstract instrumental compositions (which he liked to call 'concertos'), and the famous 'jungle' style.

Miley's 'growl' technique was central to the success of Ellington's jungle music. The trumpeter's influence is evident in the early master-piece *East St Louis Toodle-oo*, which was the band's signature tune between 1926 and 1941. Recordings of the piece made in November 1926 and December 1927 present Miley's 'growl' solo above haunting block chords scored for low reeds and tuba; this innovative texture is inseparable from its novel harmonic content, which uses a succession of inversion chords not often encountered in early jazz. Most jazz is based on 'root-position' harmonies: the 'inversions' of these chords, which lack the strong bass notes usually present, tend to sound weaker. The presence of inversions often indicates the influence of classical music. Miley's impact on Ellington's work can also be heard in *Black and Tan Fantasy*, from 1927 – a minor-key twelve-bar blues ending with a quotation from Chopin's Funeral March in allusion to the revered New Orleans funeral tradition.

Four new talents soon joined the orchestra. Adelaide Hall (1904–93) sang a haunting, wordless vocal in *Creole Love Call* in 1927, effectively functioning as an eleventh instrument. A new richness was achieved in the lowest register of the band with the arrival in the same

75, 76 The famous Cotton Club, seen here in 1938, moved from Harlem to its new venue on West 48th Street in September 1936. Ellington's residency at the original venue ran from 1927 to 1931, but he contributed music to the 'Cotton Club Parade' in 1938.

77 Harry Carney
(baritone saxophone) was
a member of Ellington's
band from 1927 to 1974.

78 The suave alto
saxophone tone of
Johnny 'Rabbit' Hodges
was a prominent feature
of Ellington's music from
1928 to 1951, and again
from 1955 to 1970.

year of baritone saxophonist Harry Carney (1910–74), who could play his oversized instrument with remarkable agility. Brilliance in the upper register was supplied by clarinettist Barney Bigard (1906–80), who also joined in 1927. Alto saxophonist Johnny Hodges (1907–70), whose suave tone had been nurtured by Sidney Bechet during his brief spell with Ellington in the summer of 1924, entered the ranks in 1928 and remained (apart from a four-year intermission in the early 1950s) until his death, as did Carney. By the time trumpeter Cootie Williams (1911–85) replaced Bubber Miley in 1929, continuing to develop the 'growl' style in the process, the band numbered twelve musicians.

Two pieces from the early 1930s brought Ellington international fame. *Mood Indigo* (1930), an example of the wistful mood pieces that formed part of the Cotton Club repertoire, was Ellington's first popular success. Originally entitled 'Dreamy Blues' and co-written by Bigard, this whimsical composition included two interesting features: impressionistic harmony, which reflected Ellington's debt to classical music, and a startlingly novel orchestration in the introductory passage, in which the trombone appears in a higher register than the clarinet, thus inverting their traditional positions. *It Don't Mean a Thing*

(If It Ain't Got That Swing), which Ellington recorded in 1932, was the first number to use the word 'swing' in its title and the debut of singer Ivie Anderson (1905–49) – who added a passage of lively scat vocals to the piece. The original 1932 recording also featured a showcase solo from Johnny Hodges, with his expressive glissandi and refined tone;

5/50 Johnny Ho

Harry Carney provided a buoyant counterpoint to the first verse, catchy riffs formed a memorable refrain, and the ending was surprising and fresh: an unresolved, dominant-ninth chord placed low in the texture and offset by a tongue-in-cheek dash of glittering sonority supplied by the Duke himself on celesta.

Now famous, Ellington and his band undertook their first tour of Europe in the summer of 1933, during which they appeared at the London Palladium. The glowing reception he received in England, from which Lambert's positive critical assessment sprang, stimulated Ellington to explore more adventurous musical territory. For some years he had tentatively demonstrated an interest in expanding the structure of his compositions beyond the confines of 78 r.p.m. recording technology, which effectively limited studio work to about three minutes. In 1931 his unorthodox *Creole Rhapsody* was recorded in two versions, one longer than the other and each occupying both sides of a disc. However, this desire to compose longer pieces in a jazz idiom did not meet with approval from Lambert, who commented three years later:

> Ellington's best works are written in what may be called ten-inch record form, and he is perhaps the only composer to raise this insignificant disc to the dignity of a definite genre. Into this three and a half minutes he compresses the utmost, but beyond its limits he is inclined to fumble. The double-sided ten-inch *Creole Rhapsody* is an exception, but the twelve-inch expansion of the same piece is nothing more than a potpourri without any of the nervous tension of the original version. Ellington has [in 1934] shown no sign of expanding his formal conceptions, and perhaps it is as well, for his works might then lose their peculiar concentrated savour.

Even so, further extended compositions followed, including *Reminiscing in Tempo* (1935), which filled all four sides of two discs and took the form of a suite made up from thematically related parts. More ambitious in terms of its musical idiom was *Diminuendo and Crescendo in Blue* (1937), another six-minute venture requiring both sides of a disc. This astonishing piece is arguably the most avant-garde product of the Swing Era. Its first section is built up from abstract and fragmented call-and-response patterns, based entirely on riffs that stubbornly refuse to transform themselves into a memorable melody on which the listener can focus; the complex, restless harmony is organized in a

79 Ellington's trombone section in 1933 (left to right): Joe 'Tricky Sam' Nanton, Juan Tizol and Lawrence Brown.

rare fourteen-bar blues pattern that passes through various keys. The second half is less adventurous, and builds to a satisfying climax by introducing more conventional riff patterns and greater tonal stability. Inevitably, perhaps, this challenging work was unsuccessful at the time. In fact, it was not until it was performed live at the 1956 Newport Festival (the USA's first regular jazz festival, founded two years earlier by George Wein) that it achieved belated recognition.

Together with these ambitious experiments, Ellington continued to produce a prolific stream of popular 'ten-inch' pieces. In 1937 he collaborated with Juan Tizol (1900–84) on *Caravan*, one of the high points of the exotic jungle style. Tizol, who had been in the band for eight years, was a Puerto Rican virtuoso on the valve trombone, which (by using a valve mechanism similar to that on the trumpet) was capable of greater agility and lyricism than the more fashionable slide trombone. A heady mixture of the jungle style and the overtly Latin elements that crept into jazz in the 1940s, *Caravan* also featured Sonny

105

80 Duke Ellington listens in admiration to Ella Fitzgerald at Birdland, New York, in 1949.

Greer's expanded percussion department: a Burmese gong, Chinese cymbal and tom-toms were added to the basic drum kit to create an exotic introduction.

Ellington's supreme command of three-minute structures culminated in several masterpieces composed between 1939 and 1941. Two pieces, both recorded in 1940, illustrate his seemingly endless resourcefulness and the extent to which his compositions had moved away from run-of-the-mill swing music, even though his band was virtually identical in size and instrumentation to conventional big bands of the period. *Ko-Ko*, another essay in the Cotton Club jungle style, shows Ellington's preference for the minor-key twelve-bar blues but avoids clichéd drumming patterns in favour of Greer's pounding tom-toms and timpani. A purposeful walking bass is provided by Jimmy Blanton, whose untimely death at the age of twenty-three deprived jazz of a major talent in 1942. (Blanton was recording a series of compelling duets with Ellington at this time that reveal him to be the most innovative bass player of his day.) 'Tricky Sam' Nanton launches into one of his best 'yah-yah' solos, and Ellington himself supplies a strikingly dissonant piano solo before the piece concludes with a daring harmony looking ahead to the 'modal' techniques of the 1960s.

Concerto for Cootie features an extended growl solo by Cootie Williams, and is notable for its rare blend of economy and inventiveness. The piece borrows the standard 'song form' of thirty-two bars,

81 Charles 'Cootie' Williams served in Ellington's band from 1929 to 1940, and rejoined in 1962 after pursuing a successful career as leader of his own groups.

popularized in Tin Pan Alley and on Broadway, in which four eight-bar phrases are organized in the pattern AABA: the three A phrases are nearly identical, while the B phrase (the 'bridge') explores different harmonies. In this instance Ellington extends the first two A sections to an irregular ten bars each, thus creating an unorthodox overall duration of thirty-six bars; he presents this self-contained pattern only once, then changes key for a contrasting central section and rounds the structure off with a single re-statement of the ten-bar opening phrase (A). Significantly, when *Concerto for Cootie* was revised in 1943 to become the song *Do Nothing Till You Hear From Me*, Ellington removed the additional bars in the A phrase to create a more conventional thirty-two-bar pattern.

By 1940, the Ellington band had taken on two new members of lasting significance: tenor saxophonist Ben Webster (1909–73) and the remarkable pianist and arranger Billy 'Sweetpea' Strayhorn (1915–67). Strayhorn created many new pieces, mostly indistinguishable in style from Ellington's, that would form the backbone of the orchestra's later repertoire. His *Take the 'A' Train* (1941), also based on a thirty-two-bar song pattern and supposedly modelled on the style of Fletcher Henderson, immediately supplanted *East St Louis Toodle-oo* as the band's new signature tune.

The American Society of Composers, Authors and Publishers (ASCAP) banned the broadcast of all their registered works from the end of 1940 until 1942 in an attempt to secure royalty payments, one of several periods of industrial action that accelerated the collapse of the big bands in the 1940s. As Ellington was a member of ASCAP, his band concentrated on works written by other (non-ASCAP) composers during this period, and the unfortunate situation helped Strayhorn to establish his reputation. In the meantime, Ellington devoted himself to major projects such as the full-length musical *Jump for Joy*, which was staged in Los Angeles in 1941, and an extended work scheduled for performance at Carnegie Hall on 23 January 1943.

For the Carnegie Hall concert, Ellington composed his most ambitious score to date: a symphonic work entitled *Black, Brown and Beige*, nearly one hour in duration, which he described as 'a tone parallel to the history of the American Negro'. Its mixed reception showed it to have fallen, perhaps inevitably, between two stools: jazz critics lamented what they saw as an absence of genuine jazz feeling, while classical critics objected to the work's loose structure. Instead of taking criticisms of *Black, Brown and Beige* to heart, Ellington only recorded extracts from the score in 1944. The work was nevertheless one of the

82 Ellington considers a musical issue with the lynchpin of
his orchestra, composer and pianist Billy Strayhorn (seated).

83 Ellington and his orchestra in 1943, the year of its first appearance at Carnegie Hall with the premiere of *Black, Brown and Beige*.

richest he ever conceived, containing all the hallmarks of his style, including Greer's jungle-style drumming and Nanton's 'yah-yah' solo in 'Work Song', and one of Johnny Hodges's most sensuous solos in the impressionistic 'Come Sunday' – a track that, perhaps more than any other passage in an Ellington work, sounds closer to a classical orchestral score than a jazz composition. From this point on, Ellington avoided the difficulties of creating jazz pieces on an extended scale by continuing to channel his energies into the suite, a form borrowed from classical music that consists of a set of individual movements linked by common subject matter. He thus created the illusion of composing pieces of extended length (his later suites could occupy an entire long-playing disc), even though the works comprised self-contained shorter sections presenting fewer compositional challenges.

Ellington's appearances at Carnegie Hall became an annual event, and invariably featured the premiere of a major composition: the *Perfume Suite* (1945), *Deep South Suite* (1946), *Liberian Suite* (1947) and *The Tattooed Bride* (1948) were all performed at the venue. *Harlem Suite* was presented at the Metropolitan Opera House, New York, in 1951 and *Night Creature* (with a full symphony orchestra, including strings and woodwind) at Carnegie Hall in 1955, but otherwise the period from 1949 to 1955 marked a low point for Ellington as the new be-bop style continued to grow in popularity. After the success in 1956 of *Diminuendo and Crescendo in Blue*, featuring a powerful twenty-seven-chorus solo by Ben Webster's successor, the tenor saxophonist Paul Gonsalves (1920–74), the band embarked on further large-scale ventures. These were invariably couched in the trusted suite format, sometimes including obvious thematic cross-references between the movements in deference to the classical composer's preoccupation with long-term structural coherence. These later works were launched through the new medium of the long-playing record rather than in high-profile live performances; among the most successful was the *Far East Suite* (1966), inspired by the band's tours of the Middle East and India in 1963 and Japan in 1964. By then, Ellington had also composed a moody soundtrack to the courtroom drama *Anatomy of a Murder* (1959), his first full-length film score.

84 Ellington's score to Otto Preminger's film *Anatomy of a Murder*, starring James Stewart and Lee Remick, was recorded between 29 May and 2 June 1959.

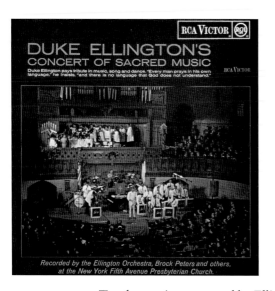

DUKE ELLINGTON'S
CONCERT OF SACRED MUSIC
Duke Ellington pays tribute in music, song and dance. "Every man prays in his own language," he insists, "and there is no language that God does not understand."

RCA VICTOR

Recorded by the Ellington Orchestra, Brock Peters and others, at the New York Fifth Avenue Presbyterian Church.

85 RCA Victor's recording of the second performance of Ellington's first 'Concert of Sacred Music', held in New York on 26 December 1965.

Two later suites arranged by Ellington and Strayhorn were based on famous classical pieces, including Grieg's incidental music to Ibsen's play *Peer Gynt* (1876) and Tchaikovsky's *Nutcracker Suite* (1892). Lovers of classical music who throw up their hands in horror at the concept of 'jazzing up' the classics should listen impartially to these skilful and ingenious reinterpretations. Jazzing-up classical music is as old as jazz itself: Jelly Roll Morton delighted in creating ragtime versions of Verdi's operatic arias in the 1910s, and Chopin's Funeral March was a staple for elaboration by early New Orleans musicians. In the Ellington-Strayhorn *Nutcracker Suite*, recognizable elements of Tchaikovsky's score are radically re-organized according to the principles of big-band jazz (chiefly riffs, call-and-response patterns and parallel harmonization) and are given coherence through the deployment of the characteristic 'sound identities', resulting in one of the finest examples of the 'Ellington effect'. In the same way as Stravinsky absorbed recognizable features of baroque and classical music into his so-called 'neo-classical' works of the 1920s and 1930s, so Ellington successfully imposed his own compositional idiosyncrasies on seemingly alien material without artistic compromise.

Ellington, who held strong religious views, regarded a series of 'Concerts of Sacred Music' as his most important achievement. The first member of the trilogy was given under the title *In the Beginning, God* in the Grace Cathedral, San Francisco, in 1965, and included material from the earlier 'Come Sunday'. The six syllables of the suite's title were represented by a recurrent six-note motif that provided a rather self-conscious source of basic thematic coherence. The *Second Sacred Concert*, which received its first performance at the Cathedral of St John the Divine, New York, in 1968, featured a dissonant passage representing primeval chaos. The third piece, entitled *The Majesty of God*, was heard at Westminster Abbey, London, in 1973 – a year before the composer's death.

In recognition of his immense contribution to jazz, Ellington was awarded the President's Gold Medal of Honor from Lyndon Johnson (1966), an Honorary Doctorate of Music from Yale University (1967) and the Medal of Freedom from President Richard Nixon (1969) at a White House party to celebrate Ellington's seventieth birthday. His success stemmed from an ability to transform mainstream jazz styles by promoting the varied characteristics of individual players, by combining these idiosyncratic instrumental voices with unusual sophistication, and by creating intellectually satisfying and constantly varied musical forms. He could, on occasion, work in as energetic and direct a big-band idiom as any other leader, as testified by his spirited album *The First Time* recorded in collaboration with Count Basie's band in 1961; he could also produce hit songs with a melodic memorability comparable to the best popular songwriters of the era. Yet the finest pieces in his prolific output (recent estimates of the total number of his compositions extend well into four figures) are distinguished by a complexity of structure and subtlety of nuance that justify comparison with the great composers of classical music. Indeed, Ellington is regarded by many as the finest American composer of the twentieth century, and the first to have rendered a distinction between jazz and classical techniques meaningless.

86 Philips's reissue of studio recordings made by the combined Basie and Ellington bands in July 1961.

CHAPTER SEVEN

Be-bop and Hard Bop

World War II affected the course of jazz history in several ways. Economic difficulties, including a severe shortage of the shellac used to manufacture gramophone records and the imposition of a hefty cabaret tax, conspired to render the big bands an extravagant anachronism. The ranks of even the most famous bands were depleted through conscription: Basie's renowned tenor saxophonist Lester Young was drafted into the US Army in 1944, the year in which he was voted best on his instrument in a nationwide poll. (He was later court-martialled for smoking marijuana.) The difficulties bandleaders faced in attempting to maintain consistency of personnel were exacerbated by the damaging series of strikes by belligerent musicians' unions, directed largely against the radio networks and involving a protracted ban on instrumental recordings; the sole exception was the 'V'-disc series, produced exclusively for export to those on active service.

The two-year recording ban imposed by the American Federation of Musicians was responsible for the music industry's singular failure to preserve on disc the new type of jazz emerging in the early 1940s, which seemed set to revolutionize the art for the future. Two Harlem clubs, Minton's Playhouse and Monroe's Uptown House, became the

87 Harold West (drums), Curly Russell (bass) and Dizzy Gillespie (trumpet) bring be-bop to the stage of Town Hall, New York, in May 1945. The concert also featured the singular talents of saxophonist Charlie Parker.

88 Minton's Playhouse, owned by Teddy Hill (far right), showcased the work of pianist Thelonious Monk (far left). Between them stand trumpeters Howard McGhee and Roy 'Little Jazz' Eldridge.

venues for informal experiments in the 'be-bop' style (named after two syllables commonly used in scat singing, and usually abbreviated to 'bop'). The movement was initially spearheaded by trumpeter 'Dizzy' Gillespie (1917–93), pianist Thelonious Monk (1917–82) and drummer Kenny Clarke (1914–85), who participated in exploratory jam sessions in 1940. In the following year, they began collaborating with the prodigious alto saxophonist Charlie Parker (1920–55).

From the outset bop was designed to be performed by small ensembles, now reduced from the sixteen players in a typical big band to a front line of between one and four instruments, plus a rhythm section of piano, bass and drums. Bop quartets, quintets, sextets and septets were an attractively economic proposition for record companies, especially in the context of worldwide post-war austerity, and several small independent labels (including Dial and Savoy) first made their names by signing musicians working in the new idiom.

Bop seemed revolutionary at the time and caused considerable controversy when the first recordings appeared in 1944. Parker told *Down Beat* magazine in 1949 that the new music 'drew little from jazz' and had 'no roots in it', but Gillespie later denied this claim in the pages of the same journal. The bop style was, in fact, rooted in the big-band techniques of the previous decade. The walking bass was retained as a harmonic foundation, and the repetitive cymbal patterns of swing music were still employed (now generally played on a single 'ride' cymbal rather than the hi-hat). Riffs remained commonplace, but were developed in two ways. As the basis for the 'head' melody with which a piece commenced and concluded, riffs gave bop themes a distinctive and fragmentary quality. At other times, riff patterns were maintained in the bass to produce a static but coherent texture that later influenced the jazz–rock movement of the 1970s. The principle of solo improvisation above a repeated sequence of chords ('the changes') remained central to the idiom. The major differences between bop and the swing style it supplanted concerned aspects of rhythm, harmony and melody.

Clarke's innovations in drumming, advanced by Max Roach (b. 1924), who also participated in the Harlem jam sessions, created unpredictable rhythmic patterns by supplying off-beat accents on bass drum and side drum that propelled the music forwards with exhilarating momentum. Heavy emphasis was often given to the second and fourth beats of a common-time bar: these 'backbeats', first used with circumspection, later became a cliché of rock and pop music. Bop drummers began to listen more closely to the melodic improvisations

89 Max Roach, resident drummer at Monroe's Uptown House, New York, during the early years of be-bop.

taking place around them, and skilfully developed the fresh rhythmic ideas of the soloists as they emerged; the drums were also promoted to the front line, providing powerful solo passages that displayed far greater flexibility and ingenuity than the performances given in the 1930s by Gene Krupa and Chick Webb.

The front-line trumpeter or saxophonist improvised solos at such speed and with such dazzling virtuosity that swung rhythm sometimes became an impossibility. The main characteristics of the new style were unpredictability and irregularity. A player's distinctive 'licks' were no longer subservient to the main melody, but became organized in abstract patterns – often of protracted length – that tended to give their solo passages a formulaic rather than memorably melodic character. A performer frequently disrupted the underlying regularity of the harmonic patterns by dislocating his melodic phrases.

90 Thelonious Monk, here shown (unusually) without one of his trademark hats.

Bop harmony was in essence simple (in fact, much bop was dependent on the twelve-bar blues progression) but developed a surface complexity that caused many commentators to believe it was based on radical ideas. The blue note flattening the fifth degree of the scale became more common than hitherto, and blue notes were absorbed into the harmony to create dissonant chords. Alternative chords were employed as substitutions to enliven well-worn harmonic progressions, many of which were borrowed from popular standards. Retaining their traditional harmonic functions for the most part, these chords were decorated by the addition of dissonances that made them sound more adventurous than they really were: this innovation affected the style of melodic improvisation, as soloists now tended to emphasize the dissonant notes of the underlying harmonies as often as the consonances. Use was also made of bitonal chords, which

118

simultaneously presented more than one conflicting harmony. In fact, most of these developments had featured in the work of Duke Ellington, whose *Cottontail* (1940) seems to look ahead to the spirit of bop in the jaunty, fragmented angularity of its main theme.

Of all instruments, it was perhaps the piano that underwent the most drastic change in style. Thelonious Monk's compositions provide the most impressive examples of bop harmonies supporting catchy themes. His eccentric manner of improvising – in which stark textures, abrupt cascades of scales and isolated stabbed notes were the essential formulae – was well suited to the abstract and unpredictable nature of bop. With a firm harmonic foundation now supplied by the walking bass, the pianist's left hand was free to explore new ideas, generally taking the form of off-beat accompanying chords that complemented the rhythmic dislocations in the drums. Many bop pianists used their right hand to imitate the driving melodic style of trumpet and saxophone, with varying degrees of success: the finest exponent of this manner of playing was Monk's protégé, Bud Powell (1924–66).

Yet no pianist could rival the fluidity, suppleness and inventiveness of the saxophonist Charlie Parker. In the early 1940s he had worked with Dizzy Gillespie in the big bands led by Earl Hines and Billy Eckstine. After the experimental jam sessions in Harlem, Parker and Gillespie made their first be-bop recordings in 1945. A year later the

91 Charlie Parker, who rose from humble beginnings in Kansas City to become the defining virtuoso of the bop movement.

92 Opened on Broadway in 1949 and named in honour of Parker, Birdland became the venue for much fine jazz in the 1950s.

93 Dizzy Gillespie's performances in Paris in the early 1950s did much to foster the growing European appreciation of the bop style.

two men travelled to the West Coast, where Parker suffered the first of his infamous drug-induced breakdowns. During the late 1940s, Parker and Gillespie were familiar figures at jazz nightclubs on 52nd Street, New York, principally the Spotlite, Onyx and Three Deuces. Most of these venues later became sleazy strip joints, as the centre for bop shifted around 1950 to Broadway venues such as the Royal Roost, nicknamed 'The Metropolitan Bopera House' by enthusiasts. In December 1949, the club Birdland, which took its name from Parker's nickname 'Yardbird' (chicken), was opened on Broadway in his honour. It was here that Parker gave his last performance in March 1955.

Parker appears to have taken his initial inspiration from Charlie Christian (1916–42), who was the first to specialize in the electrically amplified guitar. During the war Christian served in Benny Goodman's band, and was one of the early bop talents to take part in the famous jam sessions at Minton's Playhouse. His premature death from tuberculosis deprived jazz of a potentially major figure. Parker claimed that his own discovery of how to use 'the higher intervals of a chord as the melody line' dated from 1939, and this new approach to melodic dissonance was widely imitated. He became increasingly interested in the music of Stravinsky, Bartók and Hindemith, informing *Down Beat* in January 1953: 'I dig all the moderns'. Most of Parker's own compositions, however, were either heavily dependent on chord progressions originated by others or simply reworkings of the twelve-bar blues, such as *Now's the Time*, which featured a typical riff-based melody. It was the subtle detail and powerful cumulative effect of his playing, known as formulaic improvisation, that set a new standard of sophistication in jazz. His influence on later saxophonists was colossal, not only in terms of improvisational style but also on account of the raw energy in his unusual tone, which contrasted sharply with the seductive sonority of earlier swing saxophonists. The most resourceful of his direct imitators was Sonny Stitt (1924–82), who sometimes surpassed Parker in his ability to mould his motivic patterns into memorable melodic ideas.

The virtuosity of bop at first restricted the idiom to instruments that naturally lent themselves to agility, hence the predominance of the saxophone, piano and trumpet. The last played a major role because of Gillespie's stupendous technique, which allowed him to perform stunning cascades of triplets and chromatic scales, piercing high notes and startling intervallic leaps. For a time it seemed as if the more ponderous trombone would be passed by, until J. J. Johnson (b. 1924) successfully adapted a bop style of improvisation to the inherent restrictions of his instrument. With Kai Winding (1922–83), he formed a quintet featuring two trombones in the mid-1950s and secured a future for the instrument's conventional slide mechanism when it seemed in danger of losing out to the more agile valve trombone, promoted by Juan Tizol in his work with Ellington and Bob Brookmeyer (b. 1929) on the West Coast.

The dislocation of orthodox musical syntax central to the bop 'revolution' made the idiom sound unrefined and arbitrary to many conservative ears during its early evolution. Duke Ellington felt it was equivalent to 'playing scrabble with all the vowels missing', while the British poet Philip Larkin, jazz reviewer for the *Daily Telegraph* between 1964 and 1970, lamented the style's 'bloodless note patterns'. Even *Down Beat*, reviewing Parker's and Gillespie's 1945 recordings of *Be-Bop* and *Salt Peanuts*, labelled the style as 'too frantic to be worthwhile, though noteworthy in being a bit of fresh air in the otherwise too stagnant swing music of today'. Their interpretation of *Shaw 'Nuff* issued later in the same year was deemed 'still too acrobatic and sensationalistic to be expressive in the true sense of good swing'.

Cab Calloway, who had ejected Gillespie from his band in 1941 after a personality clash, simply described bop as 'Chinese music', even though Calloway had introduced Gillespie to the Afro-Cuban musical

93

techniques that exerted such a strong influence on the bop style. The 1950 edition of *Grove's Dictionary of Music*, which was not then the model of scholarship it is today, declared of bop that 'the rhythm section…plays in a chaotic manner and constantly employs South American rhythmic figures which are incompatible with those of true jazz'. Prominent examples of Latin American rhythms and harmonic colour in bop compositions may be heard in Gillespie's *Night in Tunisia* (composed in 1942 and first recorded two years later) and Parker's *My Little Suede Shoes*. Gillespie developed his own brand of big-band bop from 1945 to 1950, exploring music with a Latin flavour in collaboration with Chano Pozo (1915–48), a Cuban conga player with whom he appeared at Carnegie Hall in September 1947 – just one year before Pozo was murdered in Harlem.

The Congress of Racial Equality was founded in 1943, as the bop style was blossoming, and racial tensions in the United States had a significant influence on the socio-political attitudes of early bop musicians. In the 1930s commercially successful big-band jazz was regarded as primarily the province of white musicians, who were often better paid than their black counterparts, but a decade later bop performers (who were at first exclusively black) resolved to reclaim the creative initiative for themselves. The deliberate complexity of the new style was designed to discourage a casual audience, and even exclude undesirable players from taking part in jam sessions, while the renewed emphasis on improvisation and blues progressions restored those elements of Afro-American jazz that had largely been ignored by white bands. Members of early bop groups emphasized their difference from mainstream players by cultivating a self-conscious appearance; both Gillespie and Monk wore berets and goatees to promote their image as bohemian intellectuals rather than musicians who merely supplied dance music (as in the Swing Era). Bop set itself up as a style worthy of respect and analytical attention.

The social climate was very different in Europe, which the boppers took by storm at the end of the 1940s. Tenor saxophonist Don Byas (1912–72), one of the few figures who had progressed smoothly from swing to bop, moved to Paris in 1946, two years after he had performed with Gillespie at the Onyx Club on 52nd Street. Gillespie himself travelled to France in 1948 to appear at the first international festival of jazz, held in Nice. In the same year, Club Eleven on Carnaby Street, London, began promoting the bop style in England. Its members included saxophonists John Dankworth (b. 1927) and Ronnie Scott (1927–96). In 1949, Gillespie returned to France to attend the first jazz festival at the Salle Pleyel in Paris, where Charlie Parker, Kenny Clarke and the young Miles Davis also appeared. After their rapturous welcome, Clarke decided to remain in France; Bud Powell settled in the country ten years later.

Jazz had made considerable progress in Europe since 1919, when the Original Dixieland Jazz Band made its controversial visit to London. Paul Whiteman's orchestra came to the British capital four years later, stimulating demand for his brand of jazzy dance music. In 1926, he visited London for a second time and also took Gershwin's *Rhapsody in Blue* to Paris and Berlin. Louis Armstrong and Duke Ellington appeared in London in 1932 and 1933 respectively, by which time the European centre for jazz had shifted to Paris. The famous Hot Club de France was founded there in 1932 and the French capital was visited by Fats Waller in the same year, by Ellington in 1933 and by Armstrong in 1934. It was during the 1930s that the first significant books on jazz also appeared in Paris. Coleman Hawkins, who had joined Jack Hylton's band in London in 1934, appeared in Paris with the newly formed Quintette du Hot Club de France, the first European ensemble to reach the high standards of American jazz groups. Its suave violinist Stephane Grappelli (1908–97) and colourful gypsy guitarist Django Reinhardt (1910–53), who lost the use of two fingers of his left hand in a caravan fire in 1928 and developed an idiosyncratic technique to compensate for the handicap, created a new brand of small-ensemble jazz that looked forward to the later bop idiom.

When war broke out in September 1939, the Quintette was on tour in London. Grappelli elected not to return to France, but Reinhardt and his colleagues did. After the fall of Paris to German forces in June 1940, they began to gain first-hand experience of the Nazi Party's attempt to eradicate jazz in the interests of cultural purity. This egregious policy, which dated back to the Nazis' assumption of power in 1933, was a major hindrance to the development of first-class European jazz. Josef Goebbels, Hitler's notorious propaganda minister, viewed imported American jazz (as popular in Germany during the early 1930s as it was elsewhere in Europe) as an unclean creation of Negroes and Jews, dressed up in subversive American ideology and commercialism. Professional opportunities for Jewish musicians in Germany were severely curtailed, and in April 1938 the sale of all music recorded by non-Aryan artists was banned. Exerting his considerable power over radio broadcasters, Goebbels saw to it that authentic jazz was gradually replaced by a nondescript dance music. However, he made a point of including 'hot' jazz in the propaganda broadcasts of

94, 95 The Quintette
du Hot Club de France
featured elegant violinist
Stephane Grappelli and
flamboyant gypsy guitarist
Django Reinhardt.

96 Reinhardt's disfigured left hand compelled him to develop an unorthodox playing technique, but in no way compromised his stature as the founding father of jazz guitar.

Lord Haw-Haw (the British traitor, William Joyce) with the sole purpose of attracting listeners from enemy countries. The situation was more relaxed in countries occupied by the Nazis, including France, and Reinhardt and others were able to continue their careers in a limited fashion. Standards by Jewish composers such as Gershwin continued to be played, but their titles were heavily disguised.

A further obstacle to the flowering of jazz in Europe, less chilling but in some ways equally stubborn, was the prolonged action by the British Musicians' Union against the American Federation of Musicians, whose members were effectively prevented from performing in Britain for almost two crucial decades from 1935 to 1954. Attempts to smuggle musicians of the stature of Coleman Hawkins and Sidney Bechet into Britain in 1949 ended in an unsavoury court case. As a result, British jazz remained regrettably insular during the 1940s. An enterprising experiment in broadcasting a British version of bop in 1948 was booed and hissed, and two years later the Club Eleven in London was raided on the pretext of searching for drugs. Both incidents arose from the bitter feud between modernists and traditionalists steeped in the old Dixieland style.

97 Published in 1938, H. S. Ziegler's *Entartete Musik* ('Degenerate Music') sported on its cover a caricature of Jewish and black jazz by Nazi artist Ludwig Tersch.

98 Ella Fitzgerald's extensive 'songbook' recordings made between 1956 and 1964 remain among the best-selling vocal albums in jazz.

During the 1940s, as the history of jazz became better appreciated, early styles began to be revived. Jelly Roll Morton's 1938 retrospective inspired the rediscovery of Buddy Bolden's protégé Bunk Johnson and trombonist Kid Ory, both of whom began a series of recordings devoted to the old New Orleans style from 1942 to 1943. Meanwhile, Armstrong and Bechet enjoyed the renewed attention given to the style for which they had been largely responsible. Dubbed 'mouldy figs' by critic Leonard Feather, the traditionalists, under the leadership of scholar Rudi Blesh, staged a broadcast musical battle with the modernists, staunchly supported by the critic Barry Ulanov, in New York in 1947. Both Parker and Gillespie participated in the contest, defending the new be-bop movement. A similar debate was organized in 1952 by Leonard Bernstein at Brandeis University, near Boston, participants on that occasion including Miles Davis, John Lewis and Charles Mingus.

Part of the resistance to bop stemmed from the inescapable associa-tion between the idiom and hard drugs. While musicians had often succumbed to illicit alcohol and soft drugs during Prohibition, they turned in increasing numbers to heroin in the bop era. Parker's tragic decline from 1954 to 1955 – when, in order to finance his habit, his saxophone languished in pawn shops – became a legendary example, and his brilliance as an improviser led some naive musicians to believe that heroin had been his inspiration. As James Lincoln Collier put it:

'Heroin was a major figure in the bop movement, as significant in shaping the music as Parker himself, because one after another it took away most of the leading figures.' Mainstream musicians did not avoid addiction: Billie Holiday spent a year in prison from 1947 to 1948 for drugs offences, and was again arrested for possession on her deathbed.

Holiday (1915–59) is widely recognized as the greatest jazz vocalist of all time, a performer who revolutionized the art of jazz singing in the 1930s and exerted a powerful influence on subsequent vocalists. At her peak from 1935 to 1945, her voice (modelled on those of Louis Armstrong and Bessie Smith) was a unique blend of vulnerability, innocence and sexuality, attributes that won her a popular following.

99 Seen from the wings, Billie Holiday and Art Tatum perform at the *Esquire* jazz concert held at the Metropolitan Opera House, New York, on 18 January 1944.

100 Sarah Vaughan at a rehearsal in New York in 1950.

She had an uncanny ability to recompose well-known tunes as she sang them, creating memorable variations full of expressive leaps, pitch-bending and contrasting tone qualities. Two other female singers dominated mainstream jazz in the 1940s and 1950s: Ella Fitzgerald (1918–96) and Sarah Vaughan (1924–90), both of whom began their careers as teenage prodigies. Fitzgerald assumed the leadership of Chick Webb's band in 1939 when the hunchback drummer died and soon established herself as an unrivalled exponent of scat singing, a technique that gained renewed impetus from the desire to imitate the manner of bop instrumental improvisations. Vaughan was also a fine (though sparing) scat singer and worked with leading bop musicians in the bands of Earl Hines and Billy Eckstine from 1943 to 1945.

98

Keyboard technique continued to develop. The untimely death in 1943 of Fats Waller, who had perfected the influential Harlem stride style – even Thelonious Monk's eccentric playing was rooted in the stride school, as revealed on the occasions when he played unaccompanied – left the field wide open to the near-blind pianist Art Tatum (1909–56). Playing in 52nd Street clubs at the same time as the boppers, Tatum transformed the stride idiom out of all recognition by deploying his fluent technique across the whole range of the keyboard to create stunningly novel textures. Tatum favoured complex harmonic substitutions that were the envy of bop musicians: Parker confessed to admiring his work, which affected many later pianists.

Tatum's trio of piano, bass and guitar had been modelled on a format introduced around 1937 in Los Angeles by Nat 'King' Cole (1917–65). Cole's importance as a pioneer of small-ensemble jazz at

101 Nat King Cole's piano trio launched one of the most enduring formats in small-ensemble jazz.

102 Erroll Garner gained valuable experience deputizing for Art Tatum and first recorded his popular composition *Misty* in 1954.

the height of the Swing Era has been overshadowed by his later success as a vocalist, but his skills on the piano, influenced by the textural and rhythmic sophistication of Earl Hines, provided a link between the work of swing and bop performers. Erroll Garner (1921–77) occasionally deputized for Tatum before becoming established in his own right in the late 1940s. His inability to read music did not prevent him from evolving a highly original keyboard style based on rich textures and block-chord accompaniments. The combination of Cole's suave, laid-back melodies and Tatum's dazzling keyboard pyrotechnics shaped the distinctive style of Canadian pianist Oscar Peterson (b. 1925). He came to prominence in America in 1949 and was promoted by impresario Norman Granz (b. 1918) in his series of tours entitled 'Jazz at the Philharmonic' (which ran from 1944 to 1967), an enterprise that fostered the talents of other mainstream artists such as Ella Fitzgerald and Count Basie – and, for a time, bop stars

103 Oscar Peterson's prolific output unites technical brilliance and melodic memorability.

Charlie Parker (from 1946 to 1950) and Dizzy Gillespie (early 1950s). Peterson added a strong rhythmic beat to Cole's trio format by replacing the guitarist with a drummer in 1958. His prolific recordings offer a veritable compendium of post-1945 jazz techniques, including the so-called 'hard bop' style.

A development by a younger generation of performers, hard bop intensified bop's down-to-earth blues inflections and powerful rhythmic drive. In effect, it marked the establishment of bop as the new lingua franca of jazz, much to the consternation of those conservative critics who felt it had little in common with the 'real' jazz that had preceded it. Many bop practitioners had come to dislike the term 'bop', and made several unsuccessful attempts to replace it with the label 'modern jazz' to emphasize the validity of their position in the unbroken lineage of jazz history.

104, 105 Art Blakey
(right) recorded his *Drum
Suite* (above) in 1956, with
his Jazz Messengers and a
specially assembled
percussion ensemble.

A defining figure of the hard-bop movement was drummer Art
Blakey (1919–90), who from the mid-1950s onwards led a succession
of groups entitled 'Jazz Messengers'. Inspired by the drumming of
African musicians during visits to the continent from 1948 to 1949,
Blakey developed the rhythmic complexities of bop, exploring the
extremely difficult techniques of polyrhythm (the superimposition of
conflicting metres). As Blakey's collaboration from 1953 to 1955 with
pianist Horace Silver (b. 1928) showed, hard bop derived much of its
expressive power from bluesy elements imported from gospel music.
Silver became a major force in 'soul jazz' (otherwise known as 'funk':
neither term should be confused with modern pop–music usage), a
close relative of hard bop in which the characteristics of black religious
music continued to predominate. The hard-bop style also provided the
foundation for many accomplished performances by trumpeters
Freddie Hubbard (b. 1938) and Miles Davis, and saxophonists
'Cannonball' Adderley, John Coltrane and Sonny Rollins.

Lee Morgan (1938–72), Blakey's trumpeter from 1958 to 1961 and 1964 to 1966 and a former member of Gillespie's big band, epitomized the intense, stylish vigour of the best of hard-bop playing. His inimitable manner is exemplified by the title track and 'Blues March' from Blakey's 1959 album *Moanin'*, and his own composition *The Sidewinder* (1964), which formed the title track on the most commercially successful of all hard-bop albums. Both recordings were made on the Blue Note label, which did much to promote hard bop and soul jazz in this period. Lee Morgan's distinguished career was cut short when he was shot dead by an estranged mistress in a New York nightclub in January 1972, but by this time jazz had begun to move in an altogether different direction.

106 Lee Morgan's *The Sidewinder*, recorded in December 1963, proved to be one of the best-selling Blue Note albums on its release in 1964.

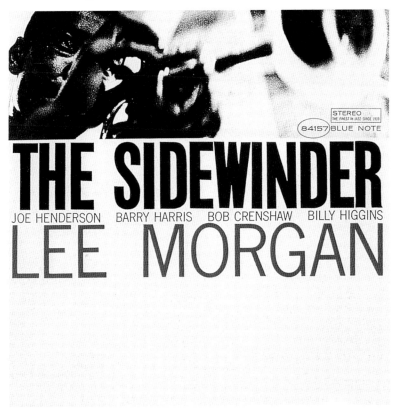

CHAPTER EIGHT

The Innovator: Miles Davis and his Influence

In August 1944, Billy Eckstine took his big band to St Louis for a two-week engagement at the Riviera Club. Some of the most adventurous bop musicians, including Gillespie, Parker and Blakey, were employed by Eckstine and they caught the imagination of a young trumpeter from the city. The eighteen-year-old Miles Davis (1926–91), who had already been playing for three years with a local group, Eddie Randle's Blue Devils, was given the opportunity to perform as third trumpet alongside 'Bird' and 'Diz'. When he moved to New York a month later to take up a place at the Juilliard School of Music, it was a matter of days before he sought out his new idols for further advice; by October, Parker had offered him work at the Three Deuces club on 52nd Street. Davis promptly quit the Juilliard, devoting himself to a career in jazz that would establish him as the most consistently innovative performer in the history of the music.

107 A studio portrait of Miles Davis taken in the late 1940s.

108 Eddie Randle's Blue Devils at the Rhumboogie Club, St Louis, in 1944. Davis is fourth from left in the back row.

From 1945 to 1948 Davis contributed to Parker's pioneering bop recordings, absorbing the principles of harmonic substitution and elaboration essential to the style after receiving tuition from Thelonious Monk. A recording session for the Savoy label in November 1945, which included a rendering of Parker's *Now's the Time*, was poorly received in *Down Beat*: 'The trumpet man, whoever the misled kid is, plays Gillespie in the same manner as the majority of kids who copy their idol do – with most of the faults, lack of order and meaning, the complete adherence to technical acrobatics.' This broadside, typical of the negative reaction towards bop in its early years, is misleading in suggesting that Davis and Gillespie were pursuing similar aims. Davis, who was not as technically able as Gillespie, evolved a refined and often restrained melodic idiom that perfectly complemented Gillespie's virtuosity. This style exerted a profound influence on the development of jazz in the 1950s.

Parker's heroin addiction had a serious effect on both his behaviour and his work, resulting in arrest, hospitalization and electric-shock therapy in Los Angeles in 1946 and an ignominious dismissal from a Chicago club in 1948 when he was too stoned to perform. By August 1948, Davis had gained sufficient experience and confidence to leave Parker and form a nine-piece ensemble, which he described as 'a collaborative experiment', with Gil Evans (1912–88). The Canadian-born composer and arranger had already revealed, in his work with Claude Thornhill's orchestra, his ability to build on Ellington's example and blend a high degree of pre-composition with sophisticated instrumental textures and adventurous harmonies. It was the encounter

109 Charlie Parker and Miles Davis during their bop collaborations in the late 1940s.

110, 111 *The Birth of the Cool*
(left) was an LP reissue of sides
originally recorded by Davis's
nonet in 1949 and 1950. Next
to Miles at one of these sessions
(below) sit alto saxophonist
Lee Konitz (centre) and
baritone saxophonist Gerry
Mulligan (right).

with Gil Evans that helped Davis to make his first significant stylistic advance: 'cool' jazz. The nonet, which also included baritone saxophonist Gerry Mulligan (1927–96), appeared for two weeks at the Royal Roost, Broadway, in September 1948 as a replacement for Count Basie's band and went on to make a historic series of recordings in 1949 and 1950. In 1957 these tracks were re-issued on the Capitol label as a long-playing album, *The Birth of the Cool*.

'Hot' was a term used in early jazz to describe those elements (chiefly syncopation, expressive tone and blue notes) that reflected the music's African influences. This type of jazz stood in sharp contrast to the polished, westernized dance music with which it competed. The nonet sessions were 'cool' in the sense that they placed greater emphasis on pre-composition and less on improvisation, an approach that demanded intellectual control and emotional restraint. Davis's own tendency to play without the addition of expressive vibrato was a crucial factor in the new sound, and one tangible way in which his style influenced later trumpeters.

Davis stated that the group aimed to reintroduce a memorable melodic dimension in jazz, and in doing so it unintentionally created an idiom with far greater appeal for a white audience than bop. Nevertheless, the Davis nonet owed much to the surface mannerisms of bop: the ensemble's interpretation of *Move*, for example, featured a head theme strongly influenced by its melodic style, and was accompanied throughout by bop drumming supplied by Max Roach. The nonet's work gained its unique character by combining angular, unpredictable bop melodies with the rich, block-chord accompaniments of big-band arrangements. In later years, Davis again collaborated with Evans to explore predominantly pre-composed jazz for large ensembles on the album *Miles Ahead* (1957), in interpretations of songs from Gershwin's opera *Porgy and Bess* (1958) and in the reworking of Hispanic material in *Sketches of Spain* (1959–60).

113 Chet Baker's 'cool' image was promoted in a series of laid-back photographic studies by William Claxton, such as this example taken in 1955.

It is ironic that cool jazz, derived from a style conceived in reaction to the white commercialization of jazz, only became a commercial success when borrowed and transformed by white musicians. Based mainly in California, the new branch of 'cool' became known as the West Coast school. Two of its most influential practitioners, Mulligan and alto saxophonist Lee Konitz (b. 1927), had participated in the Davis nonet: both were also active in the early 1950s with Stan Kenton's band in Los Angeles, which also specialized in pre-composed arrangements. In 1952, Mulligan joined trumpeter Chet Baker (1929–88) to form a quartet notable for its exclusion of the piano. This absence of a harmony instrument in the rhythm section inevitably threw greater emphasis on the ensemble's carefully con-trolled polyphony – one of the most obvious features retained from Mulligan's experience in the Davis nonet. Baker modelled his trumpet playing on Davis's understated lyricism, and his crooning singing voice made him a popular idol; a series of highly stylized photographs by William Claxton promoted him as the archetypal teenage pin-up,

141

112 Miles Davis with composer and arranger Gil Evans, with whom he collaborated in various ground-breaking experiments from 1948 onwards.

114 Stan Getz's quintet recorded this album live at Boston's Storyville club in October 1951.

presenting a new 'cool' image that has persisted in pop music to this day. The escalation in West Coast jazz in the 1950s conveniently coincided with a far greater use of jazz in Hollywood film soundtracks, increasing employment opportunities for session musicians and earning the cool style far wider publicity than might otherwise have proved possible. The idiom gained currency elsewhere through the work of tenor saxophonist Stan Getz (1927–91), another Kenton sideman, who not only nurtured a memorable post-swing style of improvisation but also did much in the 1960s to promote the craze for bossa nova ('new wave'), a blend of Brazilian exoticism and cool jazz.

An exponent of a very different brand of 'cool' was black pianist John Lewis (b. 1920), who had also served in the Davis nonet as arranger and performer. The Modern Jazz Quartet (MJQ), which he founded in 1952, comprised vibraphonist Milt Jackson (b. 1923), bassist Percy Heath (b. 1923) and drummer Connie Kay (1927–94), who replaced Kenny Clarke in 1954. Having played with Gillespie and

142

115 The Modern Jazz Quartet (left to right): John Lewis, Milt Jackson (seated), Percy Heath and Kenny Clarke.

Davis, all four had strong roots in the bop style. The MJQ, which disbanded in 1974 and then reformed in 1981 for a tour of Japan, reached a broad audience by appealing to lovers of classical music: superficially, by presenting their performances as formal concerts given in evening dress, and more profoundly by developing a formidably integrated ensemble style with Lewis's compositions as the core of their repertoire. Lewis's idiom became more widely known through the medium of film soundtrack, his scores including *No Sun in Venice* (1957) and *Odds Against Tomorrow* (1959). *No Sun in Venice* (originally entitled *Sait-on jamais*) is an impressive example of the MJQ's ability to create a workable synthesis between the techniques of jazz and classical music, even to the point of successfully tackling the complexities of baroque fugal techniques. Once again, this shows how fundamental polyphony was to the progressive textures of jazz in the 1950s.

Another West Coast musician whose work has been described as 'cool' (a catch-all term of limited usefulness) is pianist Dave Brubeck (b. 1920). Born in the same year as Lewis, Brubeck also had a classical training, but lacked Lewis's background in bop. Brubeck and his quartet achieved an intellectual respectability for jazz through a series of highly acclaimed performances on American university campuses in the 1950s. His album *Time Out* (1959) broke new ground by exploring complex metres in a jazz idiom. As Steve Race commented in his sleeve notes: 'Should some cool-minded Martian come to earth and check on the state of our music, he might play through 10,000 jazz records before he found one that wasn't in common 4/4 time.' Brubeck built on Roach's previous attempt to compose jazz in waltz metre (*Jazz in 3/4 Time*, 1956–57) by employing a wide variety of metrical schemes, including the quintuple time of the famous track 'Take Five', composed by his alto saxophonist Paul Desmond (1924–77). This piece, the first jazz instrumental recording to sell over one million copies, is also an early example of modal jazz, fusing thirty-two-bar song form and modal techniques.

In the interim, the artist who had initiated cool jazz had returned to the bop style of his early years. In 1949, Davis was one of the ambassadors of bop attending the inaugural jazz festival in Paris, after which he returned to the USA thoroughly disillusioned with the American jazz scene and drifted rapidly into the drug problems by then almost universal among bop musicians. Between October 1951 and October 1956 he recorded a series of albums for the Prestige label, including *Walkin'* (1954) and *Cookin', Relaxin', Workin'* and *Steamin'* (all four 1956). These recordings, while still owing much to the bop idiom, were characterized by an idiosyncratic intensity of colour and atmosphere, and demonstrate Davis's ability to construct lengthy solo improvisations distinguished by a high level of thematic integration and shapely control of climactic moments. The title track of *Walkin'*, performed by a septet including J. J. Johnson, Horace Silver and Kenny Clarke, showed how Davis had absorbed blues elements into his intense and sometimes sparse melodic style, foreshadowing the 'funk' of Silver's soul jazz. The piece became a standard, which in Davis's live performances was rendered at increasingly fast tempos in a style approaching the frenzy of mainstream bop.

The four albums from 1956, recorded in a spurt of activity as Davis completed his contract with Prestige before moving to Columbia, were made by a quintet comprising Davis, tenor saxophonist John Coltrane (1926–67), pianist Red Garland (1923–84), bassist Paul Chambers (1935–69) and drummer Philly Joe Jones (1923–85). Widely considered to represent the peak of both Davis's early work and the post-bop style, the performances of the Miles Davis Quintet set new standards of sophistication in accompaniment, thanks to the particularly strong rapport between the three members of the rhythm section. Over this secure foundation, a potent tension between Davis's understated improvisations and Coltrane's impassioned streams of notes lent the music a rare intensity. By this time Davis had begun to use the harmon mute, a type of 'wah-wah' mute equipped with an adjustable stem to vary the sonorities produced. By removing the stem altogether and playing close to the microphone, Davis produced a rich, breathy sound in the low register and a contrasting shrillness in high passages. These effects, which always seemed fresh in his hands, were imitated *ad nauseam* by later trumpeters as the distinctive timbre of the harmon mute acquired an unfortunate association with sleaziness.

116 Dave Brubeck and his quartet around 1960 (left to right): Paul Desmond, Brubeck, Joe Morello and Gene Wright.

117 A recording session at Columbia's New York studios in 1958 (left to right): John Coltrane, Cannonball Adderley, Miles Davis and Bill Evans.

    The quintet lost one of its members in 1956 when Coltrane left the group for a year to seek a cure for his drug addiction. Davis hired as his temporary replacement Sonny Rollins (b. 1930), who had, in partnership with Roach, developed the rhythmic complexity and thematic subtleties of Parker's formulaic improvisations. In 1957 Davis travelled to Paris, where he provided a brooding score for Louis Malle's thriller *L'Ascenseur pour l'échafaud* (*Lift to the Scaffold*) which looks ahead to the abstract themes and modal techniques of his later improvisations. By the end of the year, Coltrane had rejoined Davis and his rhythm section in New York. With the addition of alto saxophonist Julian 'Cannonball' Adderley (1928–75), the new sextet recorded a seminal album in the evolution of modern jazz, punningly titled *Milestones* (1958).

    In addition to its stature as one of the finest small-ensemble albums in the post-bop style, *Milestones* was an early landmark in the development of the modal jazz that constituted Davis's second significant stylistic innovation. If the 'cool' school had reacted against the sometimes aggressive virtuosity and structural limitations of bop, modal jazz turned away from the complexities of bop harmony. The chord changes that had formerly provided the basis for solos were now abandoned in favour of improvisation on modes (i.e. scales), although the basic overall structure of head-solos-head was for the time being retained. The essential difference lay in the lack of harmonic momentum caused by the use of strictly limited pitches, resulting in a suspension of the conventional harmonic dynamism of ongoing tension and release. Modal techniques had already been developed in classical music decades before: Debussy revived them around the turn of the century in an effort to break away from the orthodox tonal system that had dominated music since the Renaissance, and it was Davis's growing interest in later composers such as Ravel and Khachaturian that inspired him to attempt something similar in jazz. To avoid the danger of musical stasis when a single mode is applied too rigorously, Davis learnt to create variety by shifting to a different scale during the course of a piece. Davis viewed modal jazz as a challenge to melodic invention, echoing the sentiment of many twentieth-century composers who believed that the deliberate restriction of resources results in a paradoxical sense of creative liberation.

118 *Milestones*, seen here in its CD reissue, was recorded for Columbia in April 1958 and stimulated interest in the techniques of modal jazz.

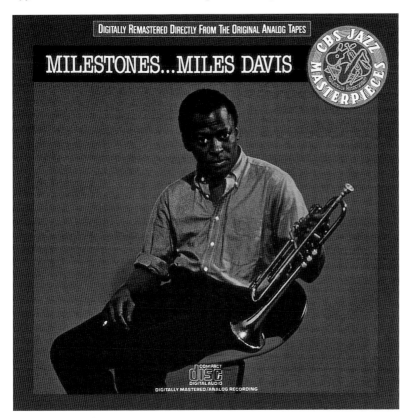

119 The inventiveness and sheer musicality of Bill Evans were potent influences on most post-bop pianists.

In the track on *Milestones* entitled 'Miles', innovative modality is perfectly fused with a conventional jazz structure. Like Ellington before him, Davis adapts the ubiquitous thirty-two-bar song form to his own ends, lengthening it by repeating the B section to create a forty-bar theme constructed in the pattern AABBA. The A and B sections are contrasted by the use of two distinct modes, and Davis remains close to the appropriate (and highly restricted) sets of pitches in his improvised choruses. Adderley and Coltrane, on the other hand, introduce more chromatic decoration; following the bop tradition of thematic allusion (established by Parker), Adderley succeeds in incorporating a quotation from Gershwin's 'Fascinatin' Rhythm' which ingeniously cuts across the underlying metre. The piece is an early example of the fade-out ending, which was later adopted by many pop musicians as a simple way of concluding their songs, but here suggests the timeless nature of modal music-making that can theoretically be extended *ad infinitum* without harmonic resolution.

The new modal approach was put to limited use in Davis's *Porgy and Bess* album, recorded in the summer of 1958, on which his interpretation of 'I Loves You, Porgy' features solo passages based on a single scale, and part of 'Summertime' is restricted to a single underlying chord. However, the most influential of Davis's modal compositions proved to be 'So What', the opening track of the sextet album *Kind of Blue* recorded in the spring of 1959. Here a standard thirty-two-bar structure is articulated by a stark modal contrast, the scale shifting abruptly up a semitone in the B section. Thematic content is restricted to repetitions of a nervous riff pattern in the bass: with the emergence of jazz-rock fusion in the 1970s, bass riffs were to be employed as a simple but essential unifying technique in the absence of a clearly defined melody. Davis's solo is a masterpiece of restraint, closely adhering to the limited notes at his disposal and generating thematic patterns with inspired, spontaneous logic. *Kind of Blue* is held in high esteem by jazz musicians because its sophisticated music was recorded with virtually no prior rehearsal.

At the piano for the bulk of the *Kind of Blue* sessions was Bill Evans (1929–80), an introverted white performer who sat somewhat oddly alongside the rest of the sextet, but who shared with Davis a deeply thoughtful attitude to jazz. Evans independently pioneered modal techniques, recording in 1958 on the album *Everybody Digs Bill Evans* the track 'Peace Piece', which was influenced by the work of Debussy, Satie and Chopin. After his brief association with Davis, Evans left to form his own ensemble in early 1959 with bassist Scott LaFaro

149

(1936–61) and drummer Paul Motian (b. 1931), possibly the most resourceful and influential piano trio in the history of jazz. The exemplary rapport between the performers is heard to best advantage in two live albums recorded at the Village Vanguard (the foremost jazz venue in Greenwich Village, New York) in June 1961, just a few days before LaFaro was killed in a car crash. Evans revolutionized jazz piano playing with his flexible left-hand technique and a far wider harmonic vocabulary than was at the disposal of most bop pianists, by his exploration of subtle cross-rhythms and by his emotional restraint and unparalleled delicacy of touch, which created a sense of wistful elusiveness emulated by many later musicians. In 1963, he conducted a bold experiment in overdubbing in the album *Conversations with Myself*, superimposing three strands of solo improvisation.

John Coltrane's departure from Davis allowed the saxophonist to develop as a leader in his own right, producing early albums such as the hard-bop tinged *Blue Train* (1957) and harmonically adventurous *Giant Steps* (1959). In May 1960, he founded a quartet featuring the talents of pianist McCoy Tyner (b. 1938), bassist Jimmy Garrison (1934–76) and drummer Elvin Jones (b. 1927). With them, Coltrane gradually intensified his style of improvising and left his bop antecedents far behind. In slow- or medium-tempo performances, he preferred an approach based on economical patterns from which he could forge cogent thematic strands; in contrast, his playing at speed was characterized by tempestuous floods of rapid notes (dubbed 'sheets of sound' by critic Ira Gitler), often alien to the underlying harmony and at times seeming to rely more on superficial effect than satisfying content.

Coltrane also showed a continuing interest in Davis's modal techniques, as revealed in the live album *Impressions* (1961), in which his irrepressible energy produced fifteen minutes of uninterrupted solo improvisation. The excessive length of his performances did not endear him to all his critics, including Davis, to whom Coltrane once admitted that he was sometimes at a loss to know how to stop playing. Davis retorted: 'Try taking the saxophone out of your mouth.' The aggressive and impassioned tone of his playing was not to everyone's taste, and it is customary to attribute the deterioration in his basic sonority in the early 1960s to drug-related health problems. Philip Larkin, one of the most conservative of jazz critics, became Coltrane's implacable opponent, lamenting his tendency to 'flagellate' themes and 'shred each chord to nothingness at breakneck speed'. In an obituary written for the *Daily Telegraph* in August 1967, sufficiently

120 Regarded by some as a spiritual guru, John Coltrane transcended his popular idolization to shape the stylistic development of younger avant-garde musicians.

strongly worded not to have been published at the time, the poet unleashed his frustrated anger:

> To squeak and gibber for sixteen bars is nothing; Coltrane could do it for sixteen minutes, stunning the listener into a kind of hypnotic state in which he read and re-read the sleeve note and believed, not of course that he was enjoying himself, but that he was hearing something significant... I regret Coltrane's death, as I regret the death of any man, but I can't conceal the fact that it leaves in jazz a vast, a blessed silence.

Coltrane's career peaked with the quartet album *A Love Supreme* (1964), which sold half a million copies in a year and celebrated the strong religious beliefs that had seen the saxophonist through his traumatic personal problems. In the opening track, 'Acknowledgement', Coltrane takes thematic economy to its most extreme level by saturating the music with a simple four-note pattern: this motif, sung elsewhere to the four syllables that make up the album's title, unifies both musical and spiritual content in much the same way as the principal theme in Ellington's *First Sacred Concert*. The final track of *A Love Supreme*, entitled 'Psalm', features an intense solo in which Coltrane 'declaims' a verbal text of his own devising by matching his instrumental gestures to the precise syllabic patterns of a highly personal poem printed in the sleeve notes. This potent song-without-words, backed up by skilful packaging which made the recording a model for later 'concept' albums, contributed to the commercial success of *A Love Supreme*. Its fashionable message, combining both spirituality and civil rights, secured for Coltrane a wide audience among the burgeoning white hippie culture in the mid-1960s and symbolized what Davis termed a 'beautiful, black, revolutionary pride'. Until his death in 1967, Coltrane grew in stature as a leading light of the emerging jazz avant-garde.

After his pioneering sidemen had gone their separate ways, Davis found renewed inspiration by surrounding himself with younger talents. In May 1963 he formed a new rhythm section comprising pianist Herbie Hancock (b. 1940), bassist Ron Carter (b. 1937) and seventeen-year-old drummer prodigy Tony Williams (1945–97). The rock steadiness of this triumvirate's time-keeping and the subtlety of its rhythmic techniques made it arguably the finest rhythm section that jazz has ever seen. Davis's second quintet, which at first included tenor saxophonist George Coleman (b. 1935), gave a fine live concert at Philharmonic Hall, New York, in February 1964, including a masterly (and largely intuitive) display of long-term structure in their extended treatment of *My Funny Valentine*. After repeating *My Funny Valentine* on tour in Japan, Davis replaced Coleman with Wayne Shorter, who was then playing with Art Blakey's Jazz Messengers. This quintet brought Davis's characteristic mixture of modal and hard-bop techniques to a peak of perfection until the group disbanded in 1968, by which time the trumpeter's attention had begun to turn towards the radical new paths offered by jazz-rock fusion.

121 The formidable Tony Williams brought post-bop drumming techniques to a peak of perfection while still a teenager.

CHAPTER NINE

Free Jazz and the Avant-Garde

To those purists who had regarded bop as a fundamental departure from true jazz, the startling freedom of modernist musicians in the 1960s seemed to represent an abandonment of all recognizable jazz elements, straining the definition of 'jazz' to its very limit. Bop had at least retained important similarities with the earlier New Orleans and swing styles, but once avant-garde performers began to reject tonality and even rhythmic continuity in their search for musical freedom, they entered uncharted and dangerous waters. Still viewed in some quarters today as an annihilation of universally accepted musical values, avant-garde jazz often appears to pose more artistic questions than it answers.

There had been several precedents for this new adventurous spirit. Blind pianist Lennie Tristano (1919–78) had experimented with spontaneous collective improvisation in his recordings entitled *Intuition* and *Digression* in 1949. The concept was developed by Charles Mingus (1922–79), who formed the Jazz Composers' Workshop in New York in 1953. In 1956, Mingus's quartet recorded the album *Pithecanthropus Erectus*, which broke new ground in its free ensemble improvisation

122 Active until the late 1970s, Charles Mingus was an unhappy musician who declared that 'jazz has too many strangling qualities for a composer'.

123 RCA Bluebird's double-album reissue of Mingus's *Tijuana Moods*, recorded in the summer of 1957, presented unedited takes alongside the truncated tracks of the original release.

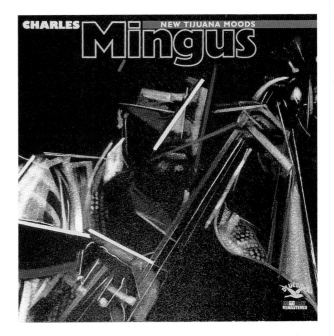

124 Roland Kirk's ostensible gimmickry belied his considerable musicality and historical awareness.

and looked ahead to the reduced importance of conventional harmonic progressions in later jazz. A virtuoso doublebass player versed in numerous styles, Mingus was in some respects a lone figure who was not influenced by trends; his work during the 1960s, especially the album *The Black Saint and the Sinner Lady* (1963), achieves a remarkable synthesis of free and pre-composed elements. His restrained forays into atonality and metrical freedom closely foreshadow the experiments of the younger avant-garde.

In 1961, Mingus's sidemen included blind tenor saxophonist Roland Kirk (1936–77), who became a respected pioneer of unorthodox instrumental techniques. Kirk resurrected two obsolete members of the saxophone family, the manzello and stritch, and developed a way of playing the three wind instruments simultaneously. He also mastered the art of 'circular breathing', which obviates the need to pause for breath. If Kirk's solo performances, in which he also played a variety of rattles, whistles and sirens, looked bizarre, the musical effects he produced were often surprisingly pleasing and were anchored in orthodox bop techniques. In a similar way other musicians attempted to achieve novel effects by using unusual instruments, including Ornette Coleman's plastic saxophone and Don Cherry's pocket-sized trumpet, though in some cases the results were little short of gimmickry.

In many respects avant-garde jazz was typical of its era, mirroring developments in other areas of the arts. By the 1960s, when avant-garde techniques had reached their peak (or nadir, depending upon the critic's sympathies) in classical music, jazz no longer lagged behind experimental concert music in terms of either technical sophistication or artistic daring. However, the absence of tonality, thematic coherence, comprehensible structure and clear rhythmic control produced depressingly uniform results from both jazz combo and symphony orchestra: sometimes only the presence of a drummer gave an indication that a work was in the jazz idiom. Even the *New Grove Dictionary of Jazz* notes that free jazz is 'best defined by its negative features'.

Although avant-garde jazz was musically radical, its artistic spirit remained true to the ideals of earlier generations of black musicians. In America civil unrest came to a head in the late 1950s when serious attempts were made to end racial segregation, first on public transport in 1956, and then in schools in 1957, a policy that gave rise to violent protests from white citizens; in Arkansas, extraordinary scenes attended the intervention of the military, and inspired Mingus to compose his 'Fables of Faubus' (named after the governor responsible for deploying the troops). These and similar experiences had nurtured a generation of black musicians who, as Larkin put it, quickly moved from using jazz 'to entertain the white man…to hating him with it'. Musical freedom became a potent symbol for the liberation from oppression that black Americans still found it necessary to demand. Jazz had, in effect, returned to the preoccupations of its early days.

The leading light of the early avant-garde was saxophonist Ornette Coleman (b. 1930), whose recording *Free Jazz* christened the incipient movement in 1960. In the previous year, he had worked in New York in a quartet with trumpeter Don Cherry (1936–95), bassist Charlie Haden (b. 1937) and drummer Billy Higgins (b. 1936) on *The Shape of Jazz to Come*. This influential album laid the foundations for an innovative style in which the focus shifted from the harmonic

125 Charlie Haden, sideman to Ornette Coleman and founder (in 1969) of the Liberation Music Orchestra, pictured here in 1992.

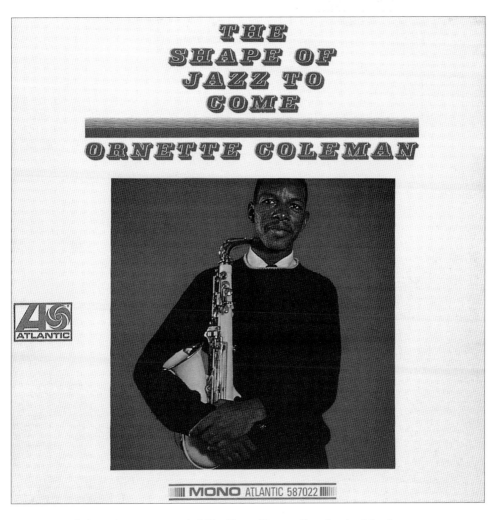

126 Ornette Coleman's quartet recorded *The Shape of Jazz to Come* for the Atlantic
label in October 1959.

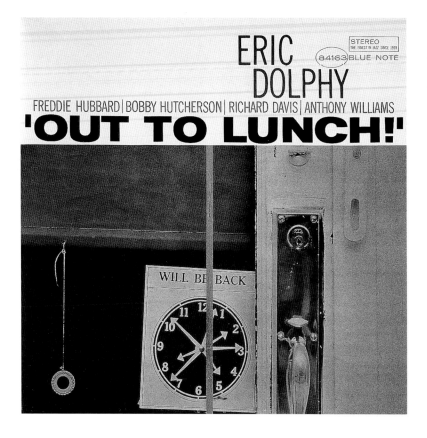

ERIC DOLPHY

STEREO
THE FINEST IN JAZZ SINCE 1939

84163 BLUE NOTE

FREDDIE HUBBARD | BOBBY HUTCHERSON | RICHARD DAVIS | ANTHONY WILLIAMS

'OUT TO LUNCH!'

dimension – a departure reflected in Coleman's decision not to include in his ensembles a piano to supply supporting chords – to melodic improvisation, whereby thematic shapes developed spontaneously and passed through freely evolving harmonic regions. Coleman commented: 'If I'm going to follow a pre-set chord sequence, I may as well write out my solo.' His music was expressionistic, in the sense that the artist's self-expression became paramount. Coleman's originality is shown by his hauntingly evocative composition 'Lonely Woman' from *The Shape of Jazz to Come*, in which material of metrical complexity is simply and effectively anchored to a static bass. Other tracks on the same album reveal the influence of the fragmentary melodic style and incongruous thematic allusions of bop, even though critics and performers alike declared him to lack musicianship and historical awareness.

160

127 Eric Dolphy's *Out to Lunch*, recorded in February 1964, featured the talents of hard-bop trumpeter Freddie Hubbard and drummer Tony Williams.

128 Versed in the techniques of several instruments, Dolphy discovered the jazz potential of the formerly neglected bass clarinet.

Free Jazz combined a second pianoless quartet with Coleman's original ensemble to create an octet, the additional personnel comprising trumpeter Freddie Hubbard, bass clarinettist Eric Dolphy (1928–64), bassist Scott LaFaro and drummer Ed Blackwell (b. 1929). Dolphy, who was also collaborating with Mingus at this time, was equally at home on alto saxophone and flute, and helped to establish versatility on more than one instrument as a central feature of the avant-garde. His Blue Note album *Out to Lunch* (1964) was a landmark in jazz flute and bass-clarinet playing. An extended group improvisation lasting well over half an hour, *Free Jazz* is at best a lively interaction of spontaneous thematic strands, and at worst little short of anarchic cacophony. The venture had considerable influence on Coltrane's album *Ascension* (1965), an ambitious experiment in instinctive and sometimes chaotic collective interplay.

Coleman went into temporary retirement from 1962 to 1965, a period during which he taught himself to play both trumpet and violin in an idiosyncratic manner – much to the disgust of Miles Davis, who lamented what he viewed as an essentially amateurish approach to instrumental technique. In his later career Coleman composed substantial concert pieces and, from 1975, worked with his electric band Prime Time. His 'harmolodic theory' (coined from a contraction of 'harmony', 'movement' and 'melody') has attempted to highlight the dual function of each instrumentalist in an ensemble as both soloist and accompanist, the breakdown in the distinction between these traditional roles having remained a central preoccupation of the avant-garde.

Both Coleman and Coltrane employed harsh, screeching sounds in the 1960s as an expressionistic device, an approach taken to extremes by the younger tenor saxophonist Pharoah Sanders (b. 1940) who joined Coltrane in the autumn of 1965. Larkin's comments on this trend have become notorious:

> It was with Coltrane, too, that jazz started to be *ugly on purpose*: his nasty tone would become more and more exacerbated until he was fairly screeching at you like a pair of demoniacally possessed bagpipes. After Coltrane, of course, all was chaos, hatred and absurdity, and one was almost relieved that severance with jazz had become so complete and obvious.

The italicized phrase (the emphasis is Larkin's) accurately identifies the style as a brand of expressionism, the first time jazz had lent itself to an artistic approach apparently at odds with its original function as an entertainment music. Larkin was by no means alone in being deeply sceptical of the new style; the *Down Beat* reviewer John Tynan described a collaboration between Coltrane and Dolphy in November 1961 as a 'horrifying demonstration of what appears to be a growing anti-jazz trend... I heard a good rhythm section go to waste behind the nihilistic exercises of the two horns'. In its May issue of the same year, Don DeMicheal drew attention to the 'technical abominations' of Coleman's saxophone playing in his defiantly entitled album *This is Our Music* (1960): his 'disdain for principles and boundaries' was deemed 'synonymous not with freedom but with anarchy', and the writer disapproved of the frequent 'yawning' passages 'filled

129 Cecil Taylor's work established common ground between the classical avant-garde and free jazz.

with meaningless notes'. The avant-garde movement was branded an 'anti-jazz' clique by critics such as Leonard Feather, for whom bop remained the central style.

Pianist Cecil Taylor (b. 1929) was as significant an innovator as Coleman, though he was not as well known. His early work with soprano saxophonist Steve Lacy and drummer Sunny Murray (b. 1937), whose style of playing departed from the rhythmic patterns of conventional jazz, was not a commercial success. Taylor's classical training and familiarity with concert-hall trends had a strong influence on his own work. His album *Unit Structures* (1966) comes close to the sound of avant-garde concert music, largely through the inclusion of an oboe in the ensemble and its abandonment of rhythmic continuity. The opening of 'Enter Evening', with its subtle combination of individual instrumental sonorities and unpredictable thematic leaps, recalls the concept of *Klangfarbenmelodie* ('sound-colour-melody') promoted by followers of the Austrian composer Anton Webern (1883–1945), renowned for the mathematical precision of his musical structures.

ALBERT AYLER TRIO

SPIRITUAL UNITY

130 Albert Ayler recorded
Spiritual Unity with bassist
Gary Peacock and drummer
Sunny Murray in July 1964.

By the mid-1960s the saxophone had become the instrument with which many leading avant-garde performers asserted their individuality, none more eccentrically than Albert Ayler (1936–70), who collaborated with his trumpeter brother Donald (b. 1942) in a series of recordings that revived elements of spirituals, folk songs and New Orleans funeral marches. Snatches of banal, tonal melody would emerge from a chaotic background of free improvisation, only to be swallowed up again in the musical maelstrom. Ayler shared several characteristics with Coltrane: an obsessive use of tiny motifs repeated over and over again and an extraordinarily powerful tone. By the late 1960s, when his record label forced him into the more commercial area of rhythm and blues, Ayler was burnt out and at the age of thirty-four he drowned himself in the East River, New York.

One of the most prolific and critically acclaimed composers in the free-jazz idiom has been saxophonist Anthony Braxton (b. 1945), who recorded an unaccompanied double album in 1968, entitled *For Alto Saxophone*. In 1966 Braxton became a member of the Chicago-based Association for the Advancement of Creative Musicians, an organization founded in 1965 by pianist Muhal Richard Abrams (b. 1930). It was typical of several musicians' co-operatives set up in the 1960s to promote free jazz, a style that was destined to remain a minority interest: similar groups were formed on the West Coast (Underground Musicians Artists Association, 1965), in New York (Jazz Composers' Orchestra Association, 1966), and in St Louis (Black Artists' Group, 1968). Chicago became the centre of the free-jazz movement, and the Art Ensemble of Chicago was established in 1969.

131, 132 Anthony Braxton (right), here playing the diminutive sopranino saxophone, introduced free jazz to Paris in 1969 (below).

This spirited quintet injected a welcome element of theatrical entertainment into the experimental improvisations of free jazz, which, by
that stage, had come close to sterility in its ceaseless pursuit of musical
abstraction. By using ethnic music and unorthodox instruments, the
Art Ensemble looked forward to later trends and reached a wider
audience on the Edition of Contemporary Music (ECM) label in the
1980s.

Another free-jazz artist who became more popular in the 1970s
was keyboard player Sun Ra (1914–93), who had formed his group
Myth-Science Arkestra in Chicago during the 1950s after an
apprenticeship in hard bop. The ensemble relocated first to New York
and then to Philadelphia. Delighting in a widely varied theatrical
presentation, the Arkestra created a richly eclectic pot-pourri of
aleatoric (random) improvisation involving as many as twenty players
simultaneously, reinterpretations of big-band classics, and essays in

133 Sonny Blount (better known as Sun Ra) began his career with Fletcher Henderson in the 1940s and later straddled numerous styles, from kitsch to the avant-garde.

134 Leading light of the emerging world-music movement in the 1970s, Don Cherry is here depicted with his trademark pocket trumpet.

exotic instrumentation – all cloaked in a 'show-biz' pseudo-mysticism. One of Sun Ra's major achievements during his long and productive career was his promotion of electronic keyboard instruments, a fashion furthered in the 1970s by the jazz-rock fusion movement.

It is not surprising, perhaps, that the audience for the most daring experiments of free jazz in the 1960s was severely limited. The idiom's lack of commercial appeal in America encouraged several prominent exponents to visit Europe, and even settle there. Taylor toured Scandinavia from 1962 to 1963, Ayler and Cherry both played in Copenhagen in 1964, and Coleman travelled around Europe in 1965. Steve Lacy (b. 1934) took his own brand of Taylor's style to Italy in 1967, fortifying it with elements borrowed from the music of his former collaborator, Thelonious Monk. Lacy moved to Paris in 1970, a year after Braxton's Creative Construction Company and the Art Ensemble of Chicago appeared in the French capital. Eager to break

135 Among Albert Mangelsdorff's innovations in trombone technique was the ability to play more than one note simultaneously, known as multiphonics.

away from earlier American styles, many European musicians adopted avant-garde techniques with alacrity. Dutch saxophonist Willem Breuker (b. 1944) formed his Instant Composers' Pool (1968–73) along the lines of American avant-garde organizations, and in 1974 founded a 'Kollektief' that presented witty and eclectic performances in which free improvisation remained an essential ingredient. West Germany was an important centre for the European avant-garde. Key figures were pianist Alex Schlippenbach (b. 1938), whose Globe Unity Orchestra also performed music written by composers of the classical avant-garde, and trombonist Albert Mangelsdorff (b. 1928). By the time these musicians were established in the 1970s, the ECM record label had begun to define its own peculiarly European brand of free jazz, which blended folk music, jazz-rock and the avant-garde.

Although the avant-garde movement had a liberating effect on subsequent jazz, opening up new avenues for exploration and providing in later years an alternative to the commercial orientation of most jazz-rock fusion, there is little doubt that in its most exaggerated manifestations it ultimately proved to be an artistic dead end. Extreme modernism is unpopular enough even in the classical concert hall, and in emulating this trend in the field of jazz many avant-garde musicians alienated themselves (sometimes deliberately and irrevocably) from a potential mass audience. Most black adherents of the avant-garde school set aside commercial concerns to concentrate on establishing a music with an artistic integrity of its own, in many respects unrelated to the classic jazz which had preceded it – and which white musicians had repeatedly hijacked to their own ends. The most outspoken and articulate proponent of a new jazz aesthetic arising from the free jazz of the 1960s has perhaps been saxophonist Archie Shepp (b. 1937), a protégé of Coltrane's who participated in *Ascension*, and whose octet album *Mama Too Tight* (1967) revealed his desire to work with a kaleidoscopic compendium of Afro-American musical idioms.

Too much freedom in music can easily lead to incoherent complexity; excessive doses of energetic expressionism can all too rapidly fail to express anything at all; the cult of originality for its own sake often produces mere gimmickry; and, worst of all, extremes of atonality, amorphousness and unorthodox instrumental noise can provide a tempting and comfortable haven for musical mediocrities. In jazz, these tendencies burgeoned at an unfortunate moment, just as rock music threatened to steal away an entire generation of younger listeners. For jazz to survive the onslaught of Beatle mania and continue to appeal to a wide international audience, an altogether different, but no less radical, way ahead needed to be forged.

136 Tenor saxophonist Archie Shepp, a sideman of Cecil Taylor's in the early 1960s, makes an appearance at the New Orleans Jazz Festival.

CHAPTER TEN

Jazz-rock Fusion and its Aftermath

'Jazz as we know it is dead,' proclaimed the front cover of *Down Beat* on 5 October 1967. The journal's decision three months earlier to include discussion of rock music in its pages seemed an open capitulation to a new popular music that threatened the continuing existence of jazz as a viable force in the marketplace. Avant-garde jazz, esoteric and forbidding, clearly presented no immediate solution to the difficult future ahead, and even internationally renowned mainstream artists such as Miles Davis and John Coltrane found themselves playing to half-empty venues. The fans' dissatisfaction with jazz derived not only from the music but also from its clean image of intellectual respectability that no longer seemed to reflect its former spirit of youthful rebellion, a mantle now assumed by the rapidly expanding rock industry.

Though a firm opponent of trends in the avant-garde, Davis still saw his record sales dwindle in the mid-1960s. His powerful label, Columbia, revived its fortunes by signing promising pop artists, while Davis's music remained a heavily subsidized luxury. He told his Columbia boss, Clive Davis: 'If you stop calling me a *jazz* man…and just sell me alongside these other people, I'll sell more.' The first indication of a change in both Davis's music and his public image came in 1968 with the release of *Miles in the Sky*. The album owed a greater debt to rock than jazz in its sleeve design, and also featured the electric guitar, electric Fender bass guitar and electric piano. In 1969, the albums *In a Silent Way* and *Bitches Brew* borrowed instruments and techniques from rock and introduced the concept of jazz-rock fusion, a style that won a vast new audience in the 1970s.

137 As jazz broadened its stylistic horizons to appeal to a youthful audience of rock fans, performers (such as Miles Davis, pictured here) adopted a mode of dress in keeping with the new market forces.

In a Silent Way, recorded in New York in February 1969, was the result of a fruitful artistic collaboration between Davis and Austrian-born keyboard player Joe Zawinul (b. 1932), who played both electric piano and electric organ. It was Zawinul's expertise on the electric piano that had first attracted Davis to the instrument. Other members of the group included Chick Corea (b. 1941), adding a third electric keyboard strand, the British electric guitarist John McLaughlin (b. 1942), drummer Tony Williams, appearing in his last recording with Davis, and saxophonist Wayne Shorter (b. 1933). Developments in recording techniques allowed the producer to reproduce short stretches of material in the form of edited loops, a procedure that opened up exciting artistic possibilities and promised a refreshing departure from conventional jazz forms.

In August 1969, an expanded line-up recorded the extraordinary ninety-three-minute double album *Bitches Brew*. Williams was re-placed by Jack DeJohnette (b. 1942), whose disruptive and constantly inventive rhythmic patterns added a disturbing quality to the music, while the three-keyboard format plus electric guitar and bass was retained. The influence of rock was also felt in the backbeats and 'straight' (not swung) rhythmic patterns of the drumming, in the abandonment of the walking bass in favour of bass riffs that could be prolonged at considerable length, and in the amplified electronic sonorities. In 'Spanish Key', a rock beat and bass riff combine to

138 Jack DeJohnette, photographed in 1990.

139 Mati Klarwein's sleeve artwork for Miles Davis's seminal double-album *Bitches Brew*, first released in 1970.

support improvisation based on scales (an approach recalling Davis's earlier modal jazz); the music was controlled by spontaneous signals from the leader. More obvious blues elements colour 'Miles Runs the Voodoo Down', which became a popular hit in a jukebox version.

The psychedelic cover artwork for *Bitches Brew* was a masterpiece of marketing strategy, combining a vivid statement of racial harmony with a strong dose of alluring voodoo. The sleeve note by Ralph J. Gleason was (fashionably) printed without upper-case characters:

> miles hears and what he hears he paints with. when he sees he hears, eyes are just an aid to hearing if you think of it that way. it's all in there, the beauty, the terror and the love, the sheer humanity of life in this incredible electric world which is so full of distortion that it can be beautiful and frightening in the same instant.

This was no longer mere jazz: as the sleeve proudly proclaimed, *Bitches Brew* represented 'directions in music by Miles Davis'.

Bitches Brew amply repaid Columbia and Davis for their jointly conceived gamble by soon becoming one of the best-selling albums in jazz history. Some commentators still criticize Davis for having 'sold out' to commercial interests in much the same way as Louis Armstrong and Nat King Cole had been upbraided before him; the debate has recently been revived by the outspokenness of Wynton Marsalis. However, it remains difficult to see how jazz could otherwise have moved out of the stalemate into which the avant-garde seemed in danger of leading it, and not be destined to remain a minority interest promoted by intellectuals and political activists. In Gary Tomlinson's words, those with different views subscribe to 'a snobbish distortion of history by jazz purists attempting to insulate their cherished classics from the messy marketplace'.

The similarities between *Bitches Brew* and rock were, in fact, superficial: even the heavy backbeats had been heard in earlier hard bop and soul jazz. The album's phenomenal and continuing popularity belies the fact that it contains some of the most challenging music Davis ever produced. Long stretches of aggressive improvisation are made coherent not by memorable melodies but by simple bass riffs and loose modal techniques, absorbed from Davis's earlier styles and here reapplied to fresh effect. This emphasis on extended free improvisation reflected the continuation of a quintessential aesthetic preoccupation of jazz, in stark contrast to the largely pre-composed nature of contemporaneous rock music. Neither mere background music nor sufficiently controlled in structure to demand consistent intellectual attention, *Bitches Brew* has remained one of the most singular and disconcerting achievements in jazz.

Davis's recordings in the 1970s failed to fulfil its considerable promise, and have been aptly described by jazz critic Stuart Nicholson as 'heavily amplified electronic gang bangs that led nowhere'; Davis's idols at this time were not the jazz masters of the past, but rock stars Jimi Hendrix, James Brown and Sly Stone. In 1975, Davis retired from public performances for six years owing to ill health, leaving the development of jazz-rock fusion to the sidemen he had assembled for his three ground-breaking albums in 1968 and 1969. One of the more virtuosic and short-lived ventures was Lifetime, founded by Tony Williams, John McLaughlin and organist Larry Young in 1969.

In 1973, Herbie Hancock explored electric-piano, synthesizer and sophisticated recording techniques in *Headhunters*, an album that eclipsed even *Bitches Brew* in sales figures. Its track 'Chameleon' became a best-selling pop single, and Hancock turned more firmly in the direction of the pop market than any other major jazz figure: his 'Rockit', from the album *Future Shock*, rose to number one in the pop

140 Herbie Hancock, house pianist to Blue Note in the 1960s, went on to win a Grammy award in 1984 for his chart hit 'Rockit'.

charts in 1983. The best of his jazz-pop enterprises are dynamic, an essential quality of the new brand of 'funk'; the worst have quickly dated. In spite of his commercial success, Hancock continued to take his work as an acoustic (non-electric) jazz pianist seriously. In 1977 he brought his former colleagues from the Miles Davis Quintet, Ron Carter and Tony Williams, together with trumpeter Freddie Hubbard to form the quintet VSOP, which five years later helped to launch the career of Wynton Marsalis. By moving between electric and acoustic jazz, Hancock typified the dual and broadminded approach of many musicians working in the aftermath of the initial fusion boom.

A more versatile development of fusion techniques was to be heard in the work of Davis's other keyboard players, Joe Zawinul and Chick Corea. Zawinul distrusted the notion of a 'jazz-*rock*' fusion, arguing

141 Chick Corea, seen here with the guitar-style synthesizer keyboard fashionable in live fusion performances in the 1980s.

142 Weather Report, featuring keyboard player Joe Zawinul and saxophonist Wayne Shorter (first and second from left).

that 'jazz–rhythm and blues' was a more accurate designation for his music (and more politically correct, as rock was a white genre and rhythm and blues a black one). In 1970 Zawinul joined forces with Wayne Shorter to found Weather Report, aptly named after the rapidity with which it leapt from one musical style to another. Weather Report flourished for fifteen years, becoming the longest surviving of the original fusion bands. Zawinul's expertise with synthesizers helped to create atmospheric and highly contrasting musical textures, to which Shorter contributed an ethereal soprano-saxophone tone that was widely imitated.

Oscillating between free improvisation and 'funky' numbers, the group was given a fresh impetus by the arrival in 1975 of the electric-bass virtuoso Jaco Pastorius (1951–87). In the 1976 album *Black Market*, liberal use was made of sound effects, such as water noises and the chatter in a black marketplace. The title track was built up from a pentatonic scale, found in some African music and therefore highly appropriate for the ethnic atmosphere, here deployed in a manner reminiscent of earlier modal techniques; 'Herandu' explored irregular rhythmic patterns of the kind initiated by Brubeck in the late 1950s.

DIGITALLY REMASTERED DIRECTLY FROM THE ORIGINAL ANALOG TAPES

WEATHER REPORT/MR. GONE

COLUMBIA JAZZ CONTEMPORARY MASTERS

143 Although it had a mixed critical reception, Weather Report's *Mr Gone* (1978) showed how free jazz could be incorporated in a mainstream fusion album.

Major success came later in the same year when the album *Heavy Weather* sold 400,000 copies on its first release. The track 'Birdland', which became a hit for the pop group Manhattan Transfer in 1979, exemplifies Weather Report's most obvious musical strengths: its ability to combine inventive pre-composed structures with earthy improvised passages and, above all, its skill in transforming otherwise banal melodies into fresh and memorable themes by using subtle and unpredictable dislocations of harmony and metre. *Mr Gone* (1978), in which no fewer than three of the finest drummers at the time participated (Tony Williams, Steve Gadd and Peter Erskine), included a free-jazz title track, a practice adopted by some of the more adventurous fusion groups. In this way, a modest future was secured for musical experimentation without compromising the commercial viability of an album.

Chick Corea had devoted his energies to a restrained form of free jazz while he was also participating in Davis's early fusion bands. His album *The Song of Singing* (1970) for the Blue Note label is an intelligent essay in a near-atonal jazz idiom: the trio's collective improvisations are sufficiently sophisticated as to appear pre-composed, and the album is a model of clarity and aural comprehensibility. After collaborating with Braxton in the short-lived experimental group

Circle, Corea formed in 1972 the first of two fusion groups under the name Return to Forever, in which he specialized on the Fender Rhodes electric piano (producing a bright, metallic timbre that now sounds somewhat dated). The track 'Spain' from the album *Light as a Feather* (1973) soon became a standard, and is typical of Corea's skill in composing buoyant and catchy melodies with intriguing rhythmic displacements. The strong Latin flavour of the early Return to Forever compositions gradually gave way to a heavier rock feeling as the membership of the group changed. In 1974 the ensemble included founder-member Stanley Clarke (b. 1951) on electric bass, Al Di Meola (b. 1954) on electric guitar and Lenny White (b. 1949) on drums. As in the case of Zawinul, Corea's compositional control over his fusion band resulted in a satisfying mixture of pre-composed structures of varying complexity, raw improvisational energy and popular melodic appeal. In 1974 he told *Down Beat*: 'What I am striving for is incorporating the discipline and beauty of the symphony orchestra and classical composers – the subtlety and beauty of harmony, melody and form – with the looseness and rhythmic dancing quality of jazz and more folky musics.' It began to appear that his desire to synthesize elements of popular and classical music was no more unrealistic after the catharsis of the fusion boom than it had been in the work of Ellington in the 1930s.

144 Chick Corea cheerfully helps out his percussionists by playing a cow-bell at the Newport Festival in 1978.

In common with other keyboard players of his generation, Corea returned to an acoustic jazz based both on fresh interpretations of classic standards and on his own compositions when Return for Ever disbanded in 1980. Like Davis, he found inspiration by surrounding himself with a younger generation of musicians who were untainted by the artistic struggles his own generation had experienced during the two previous decades. In 1986 he helped to revive interest in fusion, then adopting jazz-funk rather than jazz-rock characteristics, by founding his Elektric Band with a number of talented musicians, including bassist John Patitucci and drummer Dave Weckl (b. 1960), who gave compelling performances on the much-maligned electronic drums. Despite its virtuosity, the Elektric Band endured condescending reviews from critics who refused to accept that fusion still had a lively future. Like Louis Armstrong, Nat King Cole and Miles Davis, Corea was accused of 'selling out' – even though the band's repertoire included compositions as satisfying as any in his earlier output.

Corea recorded for Grusin-Rosen Productions (GRP), which established itself in the early 1980s as the most successful purveyor of a brand of fusion invariably deemed (and summarily dismissed as) 'popular': easy-going, tuneful arrangements with a healthy dose of funk and tasteful electronics. Though it is still fashionable to denigrate the label's catalogue, GRP has in fact produced much of interest thanks largely to the musical and entrepreneurial skills of its co-founder, Dave Grusin (b. 1934). An accomplished pianist in his own right, Grusin began his career with hard-bop trio recordings in the early 1960s and went on to work with Benny Goodman, Thad Jones and Sarah Vaughan. His compositional talents are heard to good advantage in his soundtracks (both jazz and symphonic) to such high-profile Hollywood movies as *On Golden Pond* (1981), *Tootsie* (1982) and *The Fabulous Baker Boys* (1989). Commercial success as a record executive has not sidetracked him from playing acoustic jazz, and his resourceful interpretations of standards by George Gershwin (1991) and Duke Ellington (1993) are a notable contribution to the numerous contemporary tributes to jazz's past masters.

More varied in both artistic scope and musical technique has been the eclectic work of electric guitarist Pat Metheny (b. 1954) and keyboard player Lyle Mays (b. 1953), who epitomize the new generation of American college-educated jazz musicians able to move from style to style with ease. They first collaborated on Metheny's album *Watercolors* (1977), a refined quartet performance marked by melodic

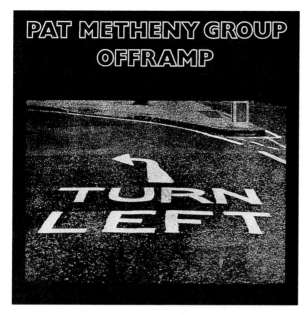

145 *Offramp*, recorded by the Pat Metheny Group in October 1981, showcased the capabilities of the powerful Synclavier synthesizer.

146 Pat Metheny performs live in 1991.

freshness and an impressionistic seascape finale, then, in the following year, formed the Pat Metheny Group with a best-selling debut album. Metheny's lyrical, effortless improvisations – strongly influenced by the innovative playing of earlier guitarist Wes Montgomery (1925–68) – and Mays's tight control of complex harmonic structures (inspired by the work of Bill Evans) created an attractive synthesis of melodic appeal and compositional ingenuity. Both performers explored electronic resources in the 1980s; Metheny made use of numerous types of guitar and the Synclavier guitar synthesizer, while Mays developed his skills on keyboard synthesizers to become one of the most accomplished and imaginative 'sonic engineers' in contemporary jazz. The stylistic plurality of the Metheny Group was strikingly shown by Offramp (1981), which, like Weather Report's Mr Gone, included a

147 Keith Jarrett, one of the most original acoustic pianists of his generation.

wildly avant-garde title track alongside music of sometimes cloying tunefulness. Among the numerous influences the group absorbed was the hypnotic 'minimalism' of American composers such as Philip Glass (b. 1937) and Steve Reich (b. 1936), which paralleled the interminably repeating riff patterns of much 1970s fusion. Minimalism also brought to jazz a refreshing dose of straightforward diatonic harmonies, which began to replace the outworn atonality and chromaticism of earlier expressionists. Following the example of Stravinsky and Copland, jazz composers learnt how to construct appealing dissonances from a handful of diatonic notes, in the process creating an economical tonal language with considerable popular appeal.

Metheny increasingly used his successful fusion group as a comfortable commercial back-up for far more ambitious musical experiments conducted with important figures from the 1960s avant-garde. In 1980 he recorded *80/81* with saxophonists Dewey Redman (b. 1931) and Michael Brecker (b. 1949), bassist Charlie Haden and drummer Jack DeJohnette. His most startling venture into avant-garde territory came in 1985 with *Song X*, on which he collaborated with Haden, DeJohnette and Ornette Coleman, who contributed unorthodox violin scraping and characteristically searing saxophone solos.

The early albums by the Pat Metheny Group were issued on the ECM label, founded by bassist Manfred Eicher in Cologne in 1969. Its distinctive brand of modern jazz – a mixture of avant-garde techniques, jazz-rock and folk music – was the first European jazz style to have a significant impact on American musicians. In addition to Metheny and Mays, other American artists to have been seduced by this heady house style have included Corea, DeJohnette, vibraphonist Gary Burton (b. 1943), Canadian trumpeter Kenny Wheeler (b. 1930) and pianist Keith Jarrett (b. 1945), who have added impressive examples of acoustic jazz to the company's catalogue. Jarrett's extended solo improvisations succeeded in blending elements of jazz, folk music and classical styles, and the ECM recording of his performance at Cologne in 1975 sold over two million copies. With bassist Gary Peacock (b. 1935) and DeJohnette, Jarrett revitalized a wide range of jazz standards in a conventional piano-trio context during the 1990s; his refusal to be sidetracked into work with electronic keyboards during the 1970s had been a factor contributing to the (at times precarious) survival of acoustic jazz in that turbulent decade. His recordings of classical music by composers as diverse as Bach and Shostakovich have won critical acclaim, and continue to erode the distinction between jazz and classical audiences.

148 Jan Garbarek has been a best-selling artist on the ECM label since its inception in 1969.

149 The final instalment in the *Codona* trilogy was recorded by Collin Walcott, Don Cherry and Nana Vasconcelos in September 1982.

The most successful European talent to have been nurtured under the aegis of the ECM label is without doubt the self-taught Norwegian saxophonist Jan Garbarek (b. 1947). In 1970 he had launched the label with his album *Afric Pepperbird*, revealing his debt to the rhetorical passion of Ayler and Coltrane. His album *Twelve Moons* was selected to be the company's 500th release in 1993, and provides an excellent introduction to its polished and atmospheric house style. An occasional sideman to Corea and Jarrett, Garbarek developed a plangent soprano-saxophone tone, ideally suited to a folk-like melodic style (appropriately suggestive of unspoilt Scandinavian landscapes). As barriers between classical music, jazz and ethnic music continued to be broken down, Garbarek recorded with Pakistani musicians in the early 1990s; and, in 1993, his haunting improvisations on the album *Officium* against a backdrop of medieval Latin vocal music performed by the Hilliard Ensemble became one of the most commercially successful crossover experiments of recent years.

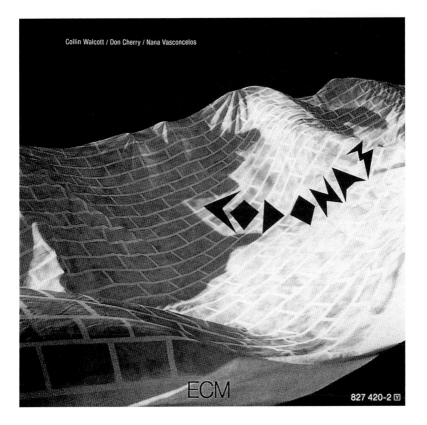

Collin Walcott / Don Cherry / Nana Vasconcelos

ECM   827 420-2 Ⓥ

'Crossover' has replaced 'fusion' as the approved term for musical ventures that transgress perceived stylistic and even cultural boundaries in an attempt to broaden the artistic perspectives of modern jazz. Garbarek's flirtation with Pakistani music is just one example in a long tradition that began with Coltrane's interest in Indian ragas and Dolphy's involvement with world music, and that gained exposure in a fusion context with the rhythmic and textural complexity of John McLaughlin's Mahavishnu Orchestra in the early 1970s. Don Cherry collaborated with Collin Walcott (1945–84) and Nana Vasconcelos (b. 1945) in a trilogy of recordings for ECM entitled *Codona*, in which Walcott played the sitar (a plucked stringed instrument) and the tablā (two small hand-beaten drums), both instruments used in traditional Indian music. Walcott's first important sitar recording came in 1969 when he participated in Tony Scott's *Homage to Lord Krishna*, and the ethnic crossover movement flourished alongside the growth of jazz-rock fusion. The percussionist Zakir Hussain (b. 1951), who specialized on the tablā, was the lynchpin of John McLaughlin's group Shakti (1973–77), in which the guitarist played a special instrument based on an Indian prototype. In the age of the global village, cross-cultural borrowings are dangerously close to becoming *de rigueur*, but the Danish bandleader Pierre Dørge (b. 1946), who founded his New Jungle Orchestra in 1980, has successfully integrated features from East European, African and Japanese musical traditions.

Crossover ventures have not been confined to Europe. In America, leading bluegrass instrumentalists have adopted the techniques of both acoustic jazz and fusion in a tuneful and buoyant idiom dubbed 'jazz-grass' or 'new grass'. The leading lights of this exuberant style are mandolinist David Grisman (b. 1945), who recorded with Stephane Grappelli in the late 1970s, banjo picker Béla Fleck (b. 1958) and guitarist Tony Rice.

As interest in acoustic jazz grew during the 1980s, a wave of 'neo-classicism' aimed to keep earlier jazz styles in circulation and encourage the preservation of a permanent repertory of masterpieces by perennially acclaimed composers such as Ellington. All styles, from Dixieland to hard bop, were subjected to reassessment by numerous groups, including the Dirty Dozen Brass Band, which resurrected the New Orleans marching tradition, and the Savoy Sultans, who brought their own version of swing to the Newport Jazz Festival in 1980. Other neo-swing bands emerged in the 1980s, while the 'cool' school enjoyed a revival in 1981 with the reunion of the original Modern Jazz Quartet. Ensembles such as the World Saxophone Quartet, founded in 1977 by Hamiet Bluiett, Julius Hemphill, Oliver Lake and David Murray, showed how the compositions of Ellington and others could be interpreted from a modern perspective. The music of Thelonious Monk was promoted by the group Sphere, founded by tenor saxophonist Charlie Rouse (1924–88) in 1979, while bop and hard-bop derivatives enjoyed the patronage of senior figures such as Sonny Stitt, Sonny Rollins and Dexter Gordon (1923–90). The last gave a moving performance as an ailing jazz musician (a composite of Bud Powell and Lester Young) in Bertrand Tavernier's film *'Round Midnight* (1986), set in Paris during the 1950s and distinguished by an Oscar-winning score provided by Herbie Hancock. Jazz in the cinema received another boost in 1988 when Clint Eastwood filmed *Bird*, a study of Charlie Parker's final years that made use of Parker's original performances as the basis for its soundtrack. By this time, the post-bop lingua franca of acoustic jazz had become sufficiently universal to be easily acquired in America through a college education.

150 Virtuoso electric guitarist John McLaughlin, who moved in 1969 to the USA, where he collaborated with Miles Davis before founding his own fusion and crossover groups.

The reputation of British jazz since the 1950s has been stimulated by the indefatigable energies of traditionalists, including trumpeter and popular broadcaster Humphrey Lyttleton (b. 1921), and the husband–and–wife duo of bop–influenced saxophonist John Dank-worth and singer Cleo Laine (both b. 1927). Virtuoso guitarist John McLaughlin collaborated with saxophonist John Surman (b. 1944) and drummer Tony Oxley (b. 1938) on the rock-tinged album *Extrap-olation* in 1969 and they went on to forge impressive reputations for themselves. In the 1980s a younger generation of musicians, including tenor saxophonists Courtney Pine (b. 1964) and Andy Sheppard (b. 1957), placed Britain firmly on the international jazz map. By absorbing the influences of Sonny Rollins, John Coltrane and West Indian music, Pine managed to reach out to a large audience. Initially influenced by Coltrane, Sheppard's playing later came closer to the sound-world of Garbarek, and he has collaborated with the innovative American pianist and bandleader Carla Bley (b. 1938). In the sphere of jazz composition, keyboard player Django Bates (b. 1960) and his eclectic big band Loose Tubes set formidable standards in the mid-1980s with their highly sophisticated responses to a wide range of

151 Andy Sheppard, whose collaborators have included Carla Bley, Gil Evans and modal-jazz theorist George Russell.

152 Courtney Pine, one of the most popular figures on the British jazz circuit since the 1980s.

musical styles and genres. Many of Bates's sidemen, notably saxo-phonist Iain Ballamy (b. 1964), have since led influential groups of their own and British jazz continues to flourish and diversify.

The most persuasive advocate of a return to traditional jazz values has been American trumpeter Wynton Marsalis (b. 1961). A child prodigy, he became the first musician to sign recording contracts for both classical music and jazz at the same time: in 1984 he distinguished himself as the first performer to receive Grammy awards in both categories. Like Miles Davis, he had both a classical training, at the Juilliard School of Music in New York, and an apprenticeship in jazz,

153

as a member of Art Blakey's Jazz Messengers; but Marsalis had a fundamentally different outlook from Davis and openly rejected fusion, which he regarded as an artistic betrayal. In 1981 Marsalis joined members of the rhythm section from Davis's 1963 quintet (Herbie Hancock, Ron Carter and Tony Williams) to play at the Newport Jazz Festival and tour Japan. Two years later his older brother, saxophonist Branford Marsalis (b. 1960), became part of the group, then called VSOP II, and went on to work with the pop star Sting. Polished interpretations of standards recorded from 1986 onwards by Wynton Marsalis with other sidemen were widely admired, and the trumpeter embarked on a systematic reappraisal of pre-fusion jazz idioms, including the 'growl' style of Duke Ellington and, in the 1988 album *The Majesty of the Blues*, the early music of his home town, New Orleans. A fluent communicator and educator, greatly envied for a supreme technical facility that makes everything he does seem dispiritingly easy, Marsalis was an inspiration to many young musicians as the American jazz renaissance extended into the 1990s.

This resurgence of interest in jazz has ensured that the musical legacy of past masters will continue to be studied and admired for years to come. In America, generous state and industrial sponsorship for jazz remains the envy of musicians from other countries: the Jazz Masterworks Orchestra of the Smithsonian Institution, Washington, DC, a group founded in 1991, was subsidized by over $300,000 from Congressional funds, and private endowments of jazz education programmes have in several cases topped the million-dollar mark. If the annual critics' and readers' polls organized by *Down Beat* are an accurate reflection of the current American scene, jazz has found a new stability as the same musicians are repeatedly re-elected in their particular categories.

Jazz in Europe, Japan, South Africa, Australasia and (since *glasnost*) Russia has made enormous strides since the 1960s, evolving into a language that has found popular appeal and intellectual appreciation in countries all over the world. Today's music is characterized by a diversity of styles – mixing elements of free jazz, the avant-garde, fusion, crossover and traditional jazz – that defy easy categorization. Meanwhile, the energetic conservation and reappraisal of the American jazz heritage by both performers and scholars is a potent reminder that this most flexible of musical idioms originated in a country where racial tension and a potent clash of musical cultures successfully bridged the gap between folk traditions and high art.

153 Wynton Marsalis performs in Vienna in 1995.

TIMELINE (durations indicated are approximate)

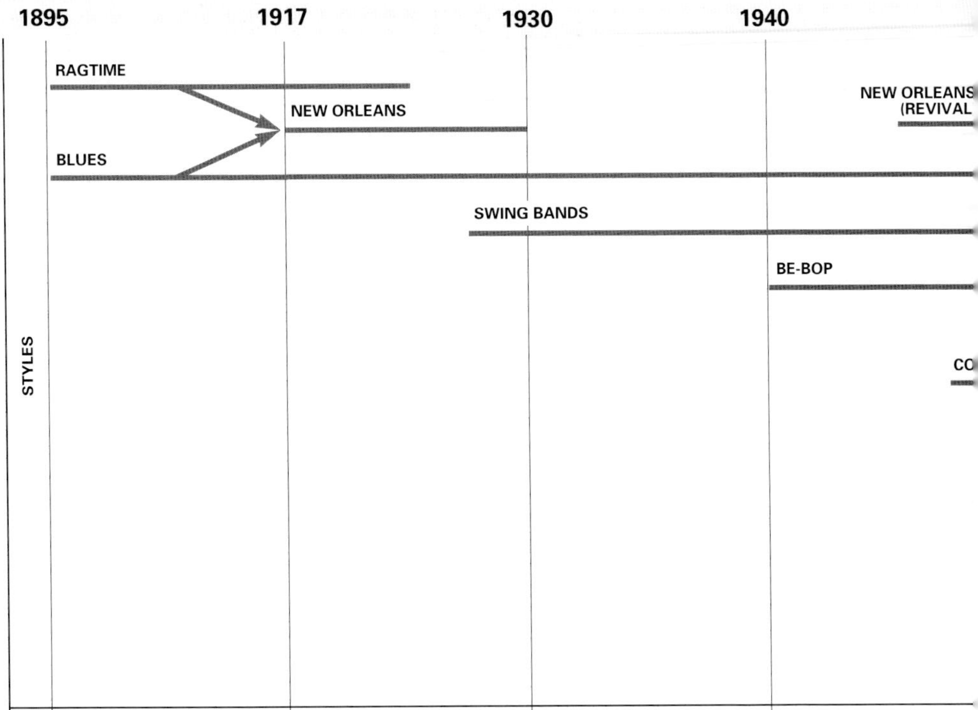

1895	1917	1930	1940

STYLES

RAGTIME

NEW ORLEANS

NEW ORLEANS (REVIVAL

BLUES

SWING BANDS

BE-BOP

CO

KEY FIGURES

Buddy Bolden	Louis Armstrong	William 'Count' Basie	Kenny Clarke
Will Marion Cook	Sidney Bechet	Edward 'Duke' Ellington	Roy Eldridge
James Reese Europe	Bix Beiderbecke	Nat 'King' Cole	Ella Fitzgerald
W. C. Handy	Fletcher Henderson	Benny Goodman	Dizzy Gillespie
Scott Joplin	James P. Johnson	Lionel Hampton	Woody Herman
John Philip Sousa	Jelly Roll Morton	Coleman Hawkins	Billie Holiday
	Joe 'King' Oliver	Earl Hines	Stan Kenton
	Bessie Smith	Hot Club de France	Thelonious Monk
	Paul Whiteman	Glenn Miller	Charlie Parker
		Thomas 'Fats' Waller	Max Roach
		Ben Webster	Sarah Vaughan
		Lester Young	

IMPORTANT EVENTS

1895 First rag published	1920 US Prohibition	1934 First book on jazz	1940–41 US broadcastin
1912 First blues published	First blues records	1935 Britain boycotts	ban
1913 Word 'jazz' printed	1923 Recording boom	US players	1942–44, 1948
1917 First jazz records	1925 Electrical recording	1936 First discography	US recording
		1937 Nazis ban jazz	bans
		1938 Carnegie Hall	1948 First jazz festiva
		concerts	Nice
			1949 First jazz festiv
			Paris
			1949 45 r.p.m./33 r
			discs

1950	1960	1970	1980	2000

RAGTIME (REVIVAL)

HARD BOP

MODAL JAZZ

FREE JAZZ

JAZZ-ROCK FUSION

ETHNIC CROSSOVER

Cannonball Adderley	Albert Ayler	Anthony Braxton	Geri Allen
Chet Baker	Ornette Coleman	Don Cherry	Django Bates
Art Blakey	John Coltrane	Chick Corea	Mike and Randy Brecker
Dave Brubeck	Eric Dolphy	Charlie Haden	Jack DeJohnette
Miles Davis	Bill Evans	Herbie Hancock	Jan Garbarek
Gil Evans	Stan Getz	Keith Jarrett	Dave Grusin
J. J. Johnson	Thad Jones	John McLaughlin	Roy Hargrove
John Lewis	Roland Kirk	Wayne Shorter	Wynton Marsalis
Charles Mingus	Lee Morgan	Joe Zawinul	Pat Metheny
Gerry Mulligan	Oscar Peterson		Courtney Pine
Bud Powell	Sonny Rollins		Cassandra Wilson
Horace Silver	Sun Ra		
Art Tatum	Cecil Taylor		

1951 First jazz film score	**1966** Dolby noise	**1970** Quadraphonic	**1983** Compact discs
1954 First US festival,	reduction	sound	**1991** Smithsonian Jazz
Newport	**1967** First Montreux	**1979** First Playboy	Masterworks launched
1958 First Monterey	Festival	Festival,	
Festival	**1969** Woodstock Pop	Hollywood	
1959 Cassette tapes	Festival		

Glossary

Cross-references to other entries are indicated by small capitals

acoustic 'non-electric', referring to sound that has not been electronically enhanced; used to distinguish an instrument from its electric version

acoustic recording a recording made before the electrical process of 1925

antiphony the spatial contrast between groups of instruments located in different positions, or differentiated by timbre (for example, brass versus reeds); in jazz, musical ideas are often passed from one instrumental group to another (see CALL-AND-RESPONSE)

arpeggio the constituent notes of a CHORD played as a melody

atonality the avoidance of a sense of key, generally through a consistent use of DISSONANCE; the idea was imported into jazz from classical music, which began to dissolve conventional TONALITY in the early twentieth century

backbeat placing a heavy emphasis on the beats of the bar traditionally regarded as the weakest (beats two and four in a four-beat bar)

ballad any slow jazz piece characterized by melodic lyricism

be-bop a style of jazz developed in the early 1940s by small ensembles, characterized by virtuosic solo IMPROVISATIONS based on complex harmonic progressions and often promoting melodic

angularity and metrical disruption

block chords the parallel motion of chords, in which all underlying parts move in the same RHYTHM as the melody; a defining characteristic of the SWING-band style of the 1930s and 1940s

blue note a microtonal flattening of the third, fifth or seventh note of the major scale, thought to be derived from African music; blue notes sound noticeably harsher on keyboard instruments, which have no pitch-bending capability

blues an improvised genre for solo voice, generally accompanied by a single instrument (for example, guitar) in CALL-AND-RESPONSE patterns, which exerted a major influence on the development of jazz; see also TWELVE-BAR BLUES

blues progression see TWELVE-BAR BLUES

boogie-woogie a keyboard version of the BLUES in which the harmonies are articulated by the player's left hand in repeated rhythmic figurations

bop see BE-BOP

bossa nova ('new wave') a jazz style popular in the 1960s, reflecting strong Brazilian influences in its restrained and lyrical use of SYNCOPATION

break a short improvised passage, usually performed by a solo instrument, inserted between adjacent sections of a piece as a means of interrupting the flow of the music

cakewalk a dance popular at the turn of the century and similar to RAGTIME in style, originally developed by black communities to parody the pretentious behaviour of white people; the name derives from the tradition of awarding a cake to the best performer of the dance

call-and-response a musical pattern of 'question-and-answer' in which a short theme is passed rapidly from one performer (or group of performers) to another in ANTIPHONY; the technique probably derived from the antiphonal singing common in slave working parties

changes the repeating pattern of CHORDS on which a conventional jazz IMPROVISATION is based

chord the simultaneous playing of different notes to create a single HARMONY

chorus in jazz, a single statement of the CHANGES on which a piece is based; solo improvisations normally last more than one chorus; the term can also describe the refrain of a popular song, preceded by a 'verse'

chromatic the 'chromatic scale' employs all twelve SEMITONES available in a single octave; thus 'chromatic HARMONY' uses CHORDS with their root notes a SEMITONE apart; the expression generally implies harmonic complexity and instability

combo slang for a small instrumental group, deriving from 'combination'

cool the opposite of HOT, usually applied to any style of jazz marked by emotional restraint

counterpoint the simultaneous combination of more than one melodic line, sometimes referred to as 'polyphony'

crossover any musical venture that 'crosses over' perceived stylistic or commercial barriers, for example, idioms that synthesize jazz and rock (see FUSION), jazz and classical music, jazz and ethnic music, etc.

cross-rhythm the combination of rhythmic patterns to create displaced accents (see SYNCOPATION) that conflict with the main pulses of the METRE

cutting contest an informal competition between instrumentalists who try to outperform each other

diatonic music restricted to the seven notes of the major SCALE

dissonance a combination of notes that sounds 'wrong' (more correctly, 'discordant'); in classical music before the twentieth century, dissonances required resolution to 'consonances'; in jazz, many milder dissonances have become standard elements of the harmonic vocabulary

Dixieland early New Orleans ensemble jazz, as performed by white groups; the term 'Dixie' refers to the southern regions of the United States

electric piano an electric keyboard instrument which imitates the sound of an ACOUSTIC piano; the metallic timbre of the Fender-Rhodes electric piano was popular with FUSION groups in the 1970s

field holler a work song (or shout) originated by slaves on American plantations

free jazz generic term for several styles of jazz, pioneered by the 1960s avant-garde, which abandon conventional harmonic, melodic and rhythmic procedures in pursuit of greater musical freedom; at times, this dissolution of traditional musical grammar has consciously symbolized the black community's desire for political and social freedom

funk a term used in the 1950s to describe down-to-earth jazz styles (those characterized by powerful rhythms and prominent BLUE NOTES), especially in contrast to COOL jazz; the term 'funk' is synonymous with SOUL jazz and should not be confused with its modern pop-music derivative

fusion a stylistic amalgamation of features from jazz and rock music, first introduced by Miles Davis in the late 1960s; see also CROSSOVER

gig slang for a professional engagement

glissando (plural **glissandi**) sliding from one note to a higher or lower note by sounding the intermediate pitches; on a piano, individual pitches between the two notes are clearly audible; on other instruments and in vocal technique a blurred effect is produced

gospel successor to the SPIRITUAL as the principal vocal genre in popular black religious music

growl a manner of playing wind instruments intended to portray the rough sound of the human voice, or a manner of 'dirty' vocal production common in the work of female BLUES singers

hard bop a loose term usually indicating a development of BE-BOP in the 1950s in which the hard-driving rhythmic characteristics and BLUES mannerisms were intensified; sometimes synonymous with FUNK and SOUL jazz, or used to indicate the importation of GOSPEL features

harmony the use of CHORDS as a basis for musical textures, generally organized into a pre-determined 'chord progression' (see CHANGES); static harmony, which tends to avoid chord progressions, is a characteristic of some MODAL JAZZ

head the statement of a theme at the opening and/or conclusion of a piece, before and/or after the improvised solo CHORUSES

homophony a single melodic line with chordal accompaniment

hot a term popular in early jazz, referring to the elements of a performance that sound 'jazzy' (such as SWUNG RHYTHM, SYNCOPATION, BLUE NOTES and expressive tone)

improvisation the spontaneous production of musical ideas by a performer, involving no conscious element of PRE-COMPOSITION

jam session an informal group IMPROVISATION

licks the characteristic (and sometimes idiosyncratic) melodic or rhythmic formulae habitually used by an individual player, sometimes referred to as 'signatures'

march a genre derived from military music, popular in America during the nineteenth century; its multi-sectional structures and simple harmonic schemes provided the foundation for RAGTIME

metre the organization of rhythmic pulses into regular stress patterns

minstrel show a comic musical entertainment, highly popular in America from the 1840s onwards, in which white performers blackened their faces and caricatured the behaviour of coloured people; in the late nineteenth century, black musicians participated in these shows and many early jazz musicians began their careers in this way

modal jazz a style of jazz, pioneered by Miles Davis and others towards the end of the 1950s, in which IMPROVISATIONS are based on MODES rather than conventional CHANGES; see also HARMONY

modes musical SCALES; in the twentieth century, both classical and jazz musicians grew frustrated with the major and minor scales that had dominated western music for several centuries, and began experimenting with less familiar modes; some of these scales were inspired by pre-classical music of the Renaissance, while others were borrowed from non-western musical traditions

mute a device inserted into the bell of a brass instrument to alter its natural timbre, generally resulting in a more subdued tone; manufactured from a variety of substances, mutes are available in numerous designs, each with a different sonorous character

novelty an instrumental genre derived from RAGTIME, featuring 'novel' figurations suggested by picturesque titles

ostinato (Italian for 'obstinate') a short musical motif subjected to more than one immediate repetition; see also RIFF

pentatonic scale any SCALE comprising five notes; pentatonic scales are widespread in non-western musical traditions and folk music

piano roll a roll of perforated paper that records a keyboard performance; when passed through the mechanism of a player piano (Pianola), an approximation of the original performance is produced

polyphony see COUNTER-POINT

polyrhythm the superimposition of conflicting METRES

pre-composition planning the structure and details of a musical work in advance of its performance, usually preserving them in the form of a notated score; the history of jazz has frequently involved a fruitful creative tension between varying degrees of pre-composition and IMPROVISATION

progressive jazz a predominantly PRE-COMPOSED big-band style promoted in the 1940s and 1950s by Stan Kenton as an amalgamation of jazz and modern classical music

race records recordings specifically aimed at the escalating black consumer market in the 1920s and 1930s

rag any piece in the RAGTIME style

ragtime an early precursor of jazz in which highly SYNCOPATED melodies were supported by solid musical structures borrowed from the MARCH; ragtime was PRE-COMPOSED, and circulated in the form of songs, piano pieces and orchestral dance music; see also CAKEWALK

reeds the generic term for wind instruments that use a reed to generate their sounds, principally clarinets and saxophones (single reeds), and oboes and bassoons (double reeds)

rhythm the temporal organization of music as patterns of weak, strong, long and short beats; rhythms are usually governed by the constraints of a prevailing METRE

rhythm section members of a jazz COMBO or big band responsible for maintaining the rhythmic and harmonic foundation of the music, and accompanying solo performers; a standard rhythm section comprises a harmony instrument (guitar,

banjo or keyboard), bass instrument and drums

riff any short, catchy OSTINATO figure; riffs were a common device in big-band music of the SWING Era, where they sometimes appeared as accompanying figures, or as the main melody; the device was retained as a prominent feature of the BE-BOP style

rip an exhilarating upwards GLISSANDO on a brass instrument

scale the arrangement of any group of musical pitches in ascending or descending order; see also MODES

scat singing singing an improvised melodic line to nonsense syllables, often in imitation of instrumental music

semitone the smallest interval between two different pitches in orthodox tonal music

side before the introduction of long-playing records, a single recorded piece was often referred to as a 'side' because it normally occupied one complete side of a 78 r.p.m. disc

sideman any player in a group other than the leader

soul a brand of HARD BOP with elements from black church music

spiritual vocal music of the black American church, developed under the influence of European hymns in the late nineteenth century

standard any song melody forming part of the 'standard' repertoire of themes used by jazz musicians as raw material on which to base their IMPROVISATIONS

Storyville red-light district of old New Orleans, traditionally considered to have been the cradle of jazz in the early twentieth century

stride piano the first important style of jazz piano playing, at its height in the 1930s; it evolved directly from RAGTIME and took its name from the 'striding' motion of the player's leaping left hand

swing type of (largely PRE-COMPOSED) big-band dance music internationally popular in the 1930s and 1940s, which gave its name to the 'Swing Era'

swung rhythm the tendency of jazz performers to anticipate the main beats of a METRE through SYNCOPATION or to alternate notes of long and short rhythmic values; both techniques propel the music forwards with a strong rhythmic drive

symphonic jazz hybrid style combining elements of jazz and classical music, popularized by Gershwin and others in the 1920s and 1930s

syncopation the accentuation of a weak beat to disrupt the expected stress patterns of a regular METRE; see also CROSS-RHYTHM

tonality the conventional system of major and minor keys prevailing in all western music until the twentieth century; see also ATONALITY

trill the rapid alternation of two adjacent notes as a decorative effect

trumpet style melodic style of piano playing developed by Earl Hines in the late 1920s

twelve-bar blues the most common harmonic progression in all jazz; it comprises twelve bars based on tonic (I), dominant (V) and subdominant (IV) harmonies, organized in the simple pattern I-I-I-I-IV-IV-I-I-V-V-I-I; the CHORDS often contain an added flattened seventh in deference to the blue notes in the melody above, and much variety has been injected into this configuration through the use of additional and substitute chords

vibrato the creation of a rich tone colour by the rapid oscillation between two notes of slightly differing pitch; various methods are used by string, brass and wind players and vocalists, but the technique is not possible on ACOUSTIC keyboard instruments

walking bass an improvised bass line that fills in the gaps between successive HARMONY notes

West Coast a style of COOL jazz originating in California during the 1950s

Select Bibliography

Budds, Michael J., *Jazz in the Sixties: The Expansion of Musical Resources and Techniques* (Iowa City, 1978; expanded edition, 1990)

Carr, Ian, *Miles Davis: A Critical Biography* (New York, 1982, and London, 1984)

—, *Keith Jarrett: The Man and his Music* (London, 1991)

—, Digby Fairweather and Brian Priestley, *Jazz: The Rough Guide* (London, 1995)

Clarke, Donald, *Wishing on the Moon: The Life and Times of Billie Holiday* (London, 1994)

—, *The Rise and Fall of Popular Music* (New York and London, 1995)

Collier, James Lincoln, *The Making of Jazz: A Comprehensive History* (London, 1978)

Cook, Richard, and Brian Morton, *The Penguin Guide to Jazz on CD, LP and Cassette* (London, 1992; third edition 1996)

Cooke, Mervyn, *The Chronicle of Jazz* (New York and London, 1997)

Coryell, Julie, and Laura Friedman, *Jazz-rock Fusion: The People – the Music*

(London, 1978)

Davis, Miles, and Quincy Troupe, *Miles: The Autobiography* (New York, 1989, and London, 1990)

Gabbard, Krin, *Jammin' at the Margins: Jazz and the American Cinema* (Chicago, 1996)

— (ed.), *Jazz Among the Discourses* (London, 1995)

Godbolt, Jim, *A History of Jazz in Britain, 1919–50* (London, 1986)

—, *A History of Jazz in Britain, 1950–70* (London, 1989)

Gottlieb, Robert (ed.), *Reading Jazz* (London, 1996)

Gridley, Mark, *Jazz Styles* (Englewood Cliffs, New Jersey, and London, 1978–85)

Hasse, John Edward (ed.), *Ragtime: Its History, Composers, and Music* (New York and London, 1985)

Hodeir, André, *Jazz: Its Evolution and Essence* (trans. David Noakes, New York, 1956)

Jost, Ekkerhard, *Free Jazz* (Graz, 1974)

Kernfeld, Barry (ed.), *The New Grove Dictionary of Jazz* (New York and London, 1988)

—, *What to Listen for in Jazz* (New Haven

and London, 1995)

Lambert, Constant, *Music Ho!: A Study of Music in Decline* (revised edition, London, 1985; original edition, 1934)

Larkin, Philip, *All What Jazz: A Record Diary, 1961–71* (revised edition, New York and London, 1985; original edition, 1970)

Lomax, Alan, *Mister Jelly Roll* (London, 1991; original edition, 1950)

—, *The Land Where the Blues Began* (London, 1993)

Nicholson, Stuart, *Jazz: The 1980s Resurgence* (New York, 1995)

Oliver, Paul, *The Story of the Blues* (London, 1969)

—, *Savannah Syncopators: African Retentions in the Blues* (London, 1970)

Owens, Thomas, *Bebop: The Music and its Players* (New York and Oxford, 1995)

Panassié, Hugues, *Hot Jazz* (trans. Lyle and Eleanor Dowling, New York and London, 1936)

—, *The Real Jazz* (trans. Anne Sorelle Williams, New York and Toronto, 1942)

Peretti, Burton, *The Creation of Jazz: Music, Race and Culture in Urban America* (Urbana, Illinois, 1992)

Porter, Lewis, Michael Ullman and Ed Hazell, *Jazz: From Its Origins to the Present* (Englewood Cliffs, New Jersey, 1992)

Rattenbury, Ken, *Duke Ellington: Jazz Composer* (New Haven and London, 1990)

Rosenthal, David H., *Hard Bop: Jazz and Black Music, 1955–65* (Oxford, 1992)

Schuller, Gunther, *Early Jazz: Its Roots and Musical Development* (New York and Oxford, 1968)

—, *The Swing Era: The Development of Jazz, 1930–45* (New York and Oxford, 1989)

Shadwick, Keith, *The Illustrated Story of Jazz* (London and Sydney, 1991)

Simon, George, *The Big Bands* (New York and London, 1968; fourth edition, 1981)

Stearns, Marshall Winslow, *The Story of Jazz* (New York, 1956, and London, 1957)

Tucker, Mark (ed.), *The Duke Ellington Reader* (New York and Oxford, 1993)

Williams, Martin (ed.), *The Art of Jazz: Essays on the Nature and Development of Jazz* (New York, 1959, and London, 1960)

Sources of Illustrations

Figures refer to illustration credits

Index